We were talking of Dragons, Tolkien and I

In a Berkshire Bar. The big workman

Who had sat silent and sucked his pipe

All the evening, from his empty mug

With gleaming eye glanced towards us;

'I seen 'em myself,' he said fiercely[1]

C. S. LEWIS

---

[1] C. S. Lewis, *Selected Literary Essays*, ed. Walter Hooper (London: Cambridge University Press, 1969), 18.

'This readable book is excellent for parents who wish to have a deep quality of communication with their children. It will also be very useful for librarians and primary school teachers, and those in churches who have responsibilities with children. The author has a firm grasp of the books of Tolkien and Lewis for children, and why they are such powerful examples of Christian writing for today's world. William Chad Newsom reminds us to savour and treasure the work of two great storytellers who were masters of incarnating Christian meaning in powerful and enduring symbols.'

Colin Duriez, author of *The C. S. Lewis Encyclopedia*, *J. R. R. Tolkien and C. S. Lewis: The Story of a Friendship*, *Tolkien and The Lord of the Rings*, *A Field Guide to Narnia*, and *The C. S. Lewis Chronicles*.

'William Chad Newsom has accomplished some very important work with this book. Many modern Christian parents do not grasp the importance of story to their children's spiritual and moral health. But not just any story will do. Using the stories of two of the twentieth century's most gifted and important story-tellers, C.S. Lewis and J.R.R. Tolkien, Newsom provides very shrewd and practical help to parents who want to grow in their love of story, along with their children.'

Douglas Wilson, author of *Recovering the Lost Tools of Learning: An Approach to Distinctively Christian Education*, *Reforming Marriage*, and the CD study series, *What I Learned in Narnia*

TALKING OF DRAGONS

THE CHILDREN'S BOOKS OF
J. R. R. TOLKIEN AND C. S. LEWIS

WILLIAM CHAD NEWSOM

CHRISTIAN FOCUS

*t*o my parents, William S. 'Sonny' and Patsy Newsom – for introducing me to great books, especially *The Hobbit*, as a child.

This book is also for all those friends and family who journeyed out to the Grande Theatre in December of 2001, 2002, and 2003, to see at last Tolkien's great story – our favourite story – come to life on the big screen, and who went out to eat afterwards both to praise and criticise: Mom, Dad, Chris, Sean, Brittany, Stefanie, Cissy, Uncle Rodney, Grandmother, Angela, Angela (yes, we have two of them!), Tom, Teresa, Kerry, Josh, Margaret, and Shawn.

Unless otherwise indicated, quotations from the Holy Bible are taken from the New King James Version, copyright © 1982 by Thomas Nelson, Inc.

Scripture quotations marked (ESV) are from the Holy Bible, English Standard Version, copyright © 2001 by Crossway Bibles, a division of Good News Publishers. Used by permission. All rights reserved.

ISBN 1-84550-106-3

10 9 8 7 6 5 4 3 2 1

Published in 2005
by
Christian Focus Publications, Ltd.
Geanies House, Fearn, Tain,
Ross-shire, IV20 1TW, Great Britain.

www.christianfocus.com

Cover Design by Jonny Sherlock

Illustrations by Dee Dreslough

Printed and bound by
Nørhaven Paperback A/S, Denmark

C✛NTENTS

Acknowledgments

*t*he book you are holding in your hands, written and edited, printed and bound, with a colourful illustration adorning the cover, is, like all books, the product of a good deal of dedication and hard work (much of it not the author's!). A lot of the time and expense is contributed by the publisher, and I would like to thank all at Christian Focus Publications, especially Willie MacKenzie and Ian Thompson, for making this possible. Thanks also to Jonny Sherlock for designing the cover and Dee Dreslough for the illustrations.

Not only did Christian Focus earn my thanks by agreeing to publish this book, they earned my admiration by retaining the services of one of the world's foremost Tolkien and Lewis scholars to edit the book. Colin Duriez is the author of many fine books on Lewis and Tolkien, all of which I commend to the reader of this little volume. In addition to his editing work, Mr Duriez provided helpful suggestions and valuable advice. For that, and for his gracious endorsement of this book, I am grateful.

I would also like to express gratitude to Professor Bradley J. Birzer of Hillsdale College for reading the typescript, and very kindly writing the foreword. I highly recommend his excellent book J. R. R. Tolkien's *Sanctifying Myth* for anyone desiring a better understanding of the Christian significance of Tolkien's legendarium.

Thanks are also due to Pastor Douglas Wilson, who graciously took time to read the typescript, and write an endorsement. He is the author of many wonderful books on theology, culture, and the family, and teaches classes on both Tolkien and Lewis at New St. Andrews College in Moscow, Idaho. For a closer look at C. S. Lewis' Narnian stories, I commend to you his *What I Learned in Narnia* lectures, available on CD.

Finally, I would like to thank my wife, Angela: for love, support, and encouragement; and for believing as strongly as I do in the storytelling culture that we are trying to build with our little ones, Grace and William – and with the new covenant blessing that we have just learned is growing within her. All glory to the Triune God.

FOREWORD

By
BRADLEY | BIRZER

Despite what has come down to us in popular memory, dragons rarely appeared in medieval literature. But, when they do arise, J.R.R. Tolkien reminded the British Academy in his famous 1936 lecture on *Beowulf*, we should be put on notice, and take our places at the watch towers. Something evil and malicious has entered the world, for the Enemy has taken a new form. Think of the words of an anonymous monk from Lindesfarne, as recorded in the *Anglo-Saxon Chronicle*.

> 793 – In this year dire portents appeared over Northumbria and sorely frightened the people. They consisted of immense whirlwinds and flashes of lightning, and fiery dragons were seen flying in the air. A great famine immediately followed those signs, and a little after that in the

same year, on 8 June, the ravages of heathen men miserably destroyed God's church on Lindisfarne, with plunder and slaughter.

To the early medieval mind, in many ways more profound than ours, one should not be surprised at such ravages after the appearance of dragons. Clearly, the Enemy had returned, a constant theme in the western tradition. And, this was only a generation after St. Boniface had created a military alliance with the Franks and evangelized the Germans, thus creating a bulwark against advancing Islamic forces. Now, the West was to be attacked from the south, east, and north. But, this is nothing new.

Indeed, the history of western civilization – in its pagan and Christian forms – has been the repeated history of declines and rises, failures and successes, corruptions and reforms. Coincidentally or, more likely, Providentially, the West seems to offer prophets and saints at the end of the declines. Indeed, through the Grace of the Logos and the light that lighteth up everyman, the West, following the supreme sacrifice of Christ, the Incarnate Word, has been built on love and sacrifice. The West was born in 480 with the death of Leonidas and his 300 Spartans at the Gates of Fire, Thermopylae. With verve and willingness, he and his men held the pass long enough to allow the Greek City-States to fortify and prepare for the Persian Invasion. When the last Spartan died, the West was born. Socrates, Plato, and Aristotle came at the very end of Classical Athens, recording and analyzing the best of their civilization. Socrates drank the hemlock, an unjust decision of his immediate generation, rather than break with the community of his ancestors. Marc Antony's men, intent on revolution and bloodshed, hunted down Marcus Cicero, the greatest of Roman republicans, and murdered him. As the magisterial Russell Kirk argued, with the death of Cicero, so fell the republic. St. Augustine witnessed innumerable invasions tearing western Rome apart. Over a thirteen-year period, he recorded his observations in *The City of God*, the most important work, outside of scripture, for the next thousand years of the West. It not only guided the medieval Church, it served, arguably, as one of the two most important sources (again, with scripture) for the Reformation. In it, St. Augustine argued that while the world, the City of Man, will experience great rises and falls, the Church, if it remains faithful to God, will continue on its sojourn, a straight line to the real City of God in our eternal life.

Each of these men, animated by the Grace of the Logos, served as an anamnesis, that which makes us remember the True, the Good, the Beautiful and, most especially, the creator of all things, Love itself, the One. It continues, of course. The blood of the martyrs built the Church. Indeed, the witness of the saints, moved by Grace, served to bring more persons to Christ, than all the rational arguments of the classical period combined. One sees it in the lives of Sts. Stephen,

Perpetua, Felicity, and Boniface, all of whom served to awaken and sanctify the western world. The martyrs of the Reformation – Jan Hus, John Wycliffe, Thomas More, and John Fisher – too were western men and exemplars of the Grace of Christ, each a reformer of a Church fallen into corruption. In the modern world, one finds the strongest arguments in the greatest Christian statesman of the eighteenth century, Edmund Burke. We should never abandon Christian society, he wrote in the 1790s, for our job is to do that which the Author of existence has assigned to us. God will take care of the rest. In his last book, *Letters of a Regicide Peace*, Burke wrote: 'The death of a man at a critical juncture, his disgust, his retreat, his disgrace, have brought innumerable calamities on a whole nation. A common soldier, a child, a girl at the door of an inn, have changed the face of fortune, and almost of Nature.' One never knows when or where Grace will arrive.

Tolkien and Lewis understood this, and they admired the martyrs and saints and even Edmund Burke. Their genius, at least in one respect, was to recognize this in the twentieth century, a century that massacred the human person in the holocaust camps, gulags, and killing fields. Tolkien and Lewis witnessed such horrors first hand in the trenches of France, as they, personally, defended western civilization. After the war, they devoted themselves to renewing and revitalizing Christian society through story and myth. As sometime Inkling John Wain wrote about the group: they were 'a circle of investigators, almost of incendiaries, meeting to urge one another on in the task of redirecting the whole current of contemporary art and life.' Lewis and Tolkien considered themselves 'Old Western Men' – men who defended a West that fought for and protected a proper understanding of the human person, fallen but bearing the Imago Dei. Each person is 'an allegory,' Tolkien conceded to his former student, famed poet W.H. Auden, 'each embodying in a particular tale and clothed in the garments of time and place, universal truth and everlasting life.'

This leads me to the wonderful book you now hold in your hands.

Mr. Newsom offers us many excellent insights into the minds of Tolkien and Lewis. Most importantly, Newsom understands the meaning of story for a Christian. God the Father spoke the universe into existence, *ex nihilo*. With Him, St. John tells us, was the Word. The Word became Incarnate, died on a piece of wood, betrayed by all of his male friends but one, and rose again on the third day. St. Paul tells us, in his letter to the Colossians, chapter 1, that Christ is the beginning, the middle and the end.

> He is the image of the invisible God, the firstborn over all creation. For by him all things were created: things in heaven and on earth, visible and invisible, whether thrones or powers or rulers or authorities; all things were created by him and for him. He is before all things, and in him all things

hold together. And he is the head of the body, the church; he is the beginning and the firstborn from among the dead, so that in everything he might have the supremacy. For God was pleased to have all his fullness dwell in him, and through him to reconcile to himself all things, whether things on earth or things in heaven, by making peace through his blood, shed on the cross.

The Word is both word and story. It is meaning and redemption. It is Grace itself, and we are each blessed to be what G.K. Chesterton called 'little words.' Even our modern English word 'Gospel' comes from an Anglo-Saxon monk at Lindesfarne, roughly 1,055 years ago. Though it comes from the Greek, 'euangelion,' Gospel literally means 'God's spell' or 'God's story.' He is the Author, and we are members of the story. We each live somewhere between the middle and the end.

For any one of us to tell stories, then, means we act as sub-creators, in the Image of God, *the* Creator. Stories – along with words – contain immense power, and we should use that power, aided by Grace, wisely. When we do so, Newsom reminds us, we pursue the Good, the True, and the Beautiful. And, the words we read – for good or ill – have power. Michael O'Brien, a Canadian author and artist, has recently described each book as akin to a soul. It goes into the world; some to do good, others to do ill. Therefore, we must always be vigilant – as parents, teachers, and Christians – about the books we read, the books our children read, and the books our friends read.

As long as we rely on the Grace of the Logos, we will do well and good, and the whole of western and Christian civilization may very well be renewed, refreshed, and reformed. Armed with imagination and devout dedication to Christ, Tolkien, Lewis, and Newsom are leading the way. Swords drawn, let us follow ... and slay dragons.

> Bradley J. Birzer is Russell Amos Kirk Chair in History, Hillsdale College, Michigan. He is author of *J.R.R. Tolkien's Sanctifying Myth: Understanding Middle-earth* (2003); and *Sanctifying the World: The Augustinian Life and Mind of Christopher Dawson* (late 2005). He and his wife, Dedra, have four children.

PREFACE

If you sometimes read into my books what I did not know I had put there, neither of us need be surprised, for greater readers have doubtless done the same to far greater authors...Perhaps a book ought to have more meanings than the writer intends?[2]

C. S. LEWIS

the record-breaking success of Peter Jackson's *The Lord of the Rings* films has turned the movie world upside down in the last few years. Jackson's adaptation of J. R. R. Tolkien's book spawned an entire industry of ancillary products: action figures, collectible cards, glassware, and more. Many Christian parents, perhaps unfamiliar with Tolkien's stories, suddenly found themselves in a culture awash in references to, and images of, Tolkien's world of Middle-earth. Furthermore, we are soon to see the first film adaptation of *The Chronicles of Narnia*, written by Tolkien's

---

[2] C. S. Lewis, *Letters of C. S. Lewis*, ed. W. H. Lewis (San Diego: Harcourt, Inc., 1966, 1988), 487.

friend, C. S. Lewis. The excitement generated by this upcoming movie series promises an impact on pop culture comparable to the *Rings* films.

But again, many Christian parents know little, if anything, of these strange fairy-tales. On the one hand, 'fairy-tales' are widely considered (at best) 'children's literature', yet many have noticed that *The Lord of the Rings* is enjoyed by at least as many adults as children. Some have written the book off as merely another corner of the universe inhabited by 'Trekkies' (fans of *Star Trek*), and, consequently, of little importance, depending entirely on whether you like that sort of thing. Others are actively hostile to fairy-tales, determined to keep their children's heads out of the clouds, and their eyes firmly fixed on the Real World, however that may be defined. Such parents despise mythology, poetry, even fiction itself, perhaps, as somehow un-Christian. Still, some may have heard something about Tolkien's Christian faith, or that Lewis was a famous convert to Christ from atheism who also wrote popular books of Christian theology.

This book is for those who want to know more. It is written in the hope that those already acquainted with the writings of Tolkien and Lewis will find the reading of it worthwhile; but it is primarily an introduction to those new to the books: the non-specialist parents who care about what their children read and watch. For this reason, and because I want to especially emphasise the role of fathers and mothers as storytellers, this book will focus on the children's writings of these two great authors. It will serve, I hope, as an introduction for those parents trying to understand the place of those stories (and perhaps of any stories) in the lives of their children.

As we read through these stories, we shall be looking for what some have called the three aspects of the good life: goodness, truth, and beauty. The pursuit of this trinity of virtues is a pursuit the Bible itself commands: 'Finally, brethren, whatever things are true, whatever things are noble, whatever things are just, whatever things are pure, whatever things are lovely, whatever things are of good report, if there is any virtue and if there is anything praiseworthy – meditate on these things'.[3] We shall seek these glimpses of goodness, truth, and beauty, knowing that some of them were intended by Lewis and Tolkien, while others, perhaps, were not. We remember Lewis's words as quoted above: 'Perhaps a book ought to have more meanings than the writer intends…' This does not suggest that the meaning is relative, or that there is no meaning beyond what each reader finds there. Rather, it is a recognition that we do not know everything, and that, if a story is successful in portraying reality as God made it, it will sometimes do so in ways the storyteller did not, and maybe could not, imagine.

Along the way, suggestions are offered to help you and your children to get the most out of these

[3] Philippians 4:8

great tales. Lewis once wrote a snippet of poetry in which he mentions 'talking of dragons' with Tolkien.[4] The suggestion of this book, strange though it may seem to some, is that the Christian parent *must* talk about dragons to his children – if he wants them to be godly children who love the Bible, and who trust God. This is a family book, then, one that can be used alongside your copy of *The Hobbit* or *The Chronicles of Narnia*, but it is, first and foremost, an encouragement to actually read, for yourself and for the covenant blessings God has entrusted to you, the children's stories of J. R. R. Tolkien and C. S. Lewis.

---

[4] The episode he describes in that poem is fictional, though there is no doubt that the two friends often talked not only of dragons but every other kind of mythological and legendary creature.

CHAPTER ⊕NE

FAMILY HIST⊕RY: ST⊕RIES AND THEIR PLACE IN THE ST⊕RY

> *I would venture to say that approaching the Christian Story from this direction, it has long been my feeling (a joyous feeling) that God redeemed the corrupt making-creatures, men, in a way fitting to this aspect, as to others, of their strange nature…There is no tale ever told that men would rather find was true, and none which so many sceptical men have accepted as true on its own merits. For the Art of it has the supremely convincing tone of Primary Art, that is, of Creation. To reject it leads either to sadness or to wrath.*[5]

> ### J. R. R. tolkien

FOR Christians, the Bible is not merely a religious guidebook, but the family history of our people. Those who would know and understand this history must seek in one place

---

[5] J. R. R. Tolkien, *Poems and Stories* (Boston: Houghton Mifflin Company, 1994), 179.

only, and to our surprised modern minds, that place is a book. Therefore, reading is essential for the Christian. The option of not being 'into' reading is not given us. Perhaps, as you are reading at this very moment, very little needs to be said about this. God, who could have waited until the age of cable and satellite to reveal His purpose, and displayed his Story on plasma and flat screen, chose to do so in a book. We must read, then, and we cannot read only the Bible – not if we hope to understand the Bible, that is. The New Testament, for instance, records events that took place in the Classical Roman world. Allusions, references, even quotes, abound in the Scriptures, which we cannot understand without at least some knowledge of Classical literature and history. The same can be said of the ancient world of the Hebrews and the cultures that surrounded them. Though God no longer breathed out the Scriptures after the first century, He did not cease to work among His people, but continued writing their stories as a continuation of His. The period of the early Church Fathers – the Patristic, as well as the Medieval, Reformation, and modern eras, are all part of our family history. God has given the Church teachers,[6] and we should not stop listening to them just because they have died. The link to our dead teachers is their writings.

So we must read, joining the great conversation of history, but because there are so many choices,

6 Ephesians 4:11

we must take care in selecting our books. The fact that you have a book open does not mean you are engaged in the great conversation, if say, Danielle Steele wrote that book. If the last 'Great Book' you read was the latest installment of *Left Behind*, it is time for a re-sorting of priorities (no, I'm not saying it's a sin to read *Left Behind*, but I am saying that *Left Behind*, unlike some books, is something you really can take or leave). Perhaps you really do spend a lot of time reading. Take a quick inventory of the kinds of books you read, however. Hollywood gossip magazines? Cheap romance novels? Tabloids?

Devotional books? Maybe you would never read Dan Brown or *The National Enquirer*, but you limit yourself to books on Christian living, or biblical commentaries. Do you read fiction at all? As we begin our book on two great writers of fairy tales and poetry, I want to suggest that, to be a biblical Christian, *you must both read and enjoy poetry and fairy tales*. I know this statement sounds, to many readers, as shocking and ridiculous as if I had claimed that a steady diet of *Star Trek* is necessary for sanctification, but there is a difference. Listen to the words of author and poet Doug Jones and be sure to check your blood pressure when you are done:

> Though I have heard it too many times, I am still pierced through when I hear Christian parents glibly proclaiming that they don't want their children to hear fairy tales or fiction of any sort.

It sounds like a certain death sentence. It sounds
like the parent is saying, 'I'm really hoping to raise
imbeciles and perverts to the glory of God.'[7]

Can he be serious? It is certainly a strong statement
to make about a mere literary preference. In
another place, Jones made this declaration:
'Though I couldn't prove it in an ecclesiastical
court, I'm beginning to suspect that parents
who don't enjoy fiction must have some serious
spiritual problem lurking about, either in a very
distorted view of spirituality or in a rejection of
beauty. They are like the person who ungratefully
refuses to delight in God's handiwork in nature.
Time will tell in the lives of their children.'[8]

But it is not enough to make controversial
statements: reasons must be provided, and to that
task we now turn. Much could be said here about
the cultural well-being of children (and adults),
the need to listen to the wisdom of others, and
broadening our understanding by reading outside
of our comfort zones. Though there is truth in all
of these, the case for fairy tales and poetry can
be made much more simply, by an appeal to the
Scriptures themselves.

To begin with, let us consider the various kinds
of literature found in the Bible. History is the

---

[7] Douglas Jones, "Imaginative Succession," *Credenda Agenda*,
Volume 13, Issue 2.

[8] Douglas Jones and Douglas Wilson, *Angels in the Architecture:
A Protestant Vision for Middle Earth* (Moscow, Idaho: Canon Press,
1998), 124-125. I am indebted to Jones and Wilson (both for this
fine book as well as other writings) throughout this chapter.

dominant form: Scripture is a record of events that took place at particular times and places. History is a record of the stories of a people, and the Bible records for us the tales of God's people. Adam, Noah, Abraham, Moses, David, the Prophets, John the Baptist, Jesus and His apostles – all are characters in the story of redemptive history, and all are a part of the family history of Christians.

The Bible, then, is a story, or The Story, we should say. But that Story is written down in a variety of forms, images, and narratives. The Old Testament books of Job, Psalms, Proverbs, Ecclesiastes, and Song of Solomon are regarded as books of poetry – and notice that this section of God's Word includes both the longest book in the Bible (Psalms) and the longest chapter (Psalm 119). Obviously, God delights in poetry, and this is reason enough for Christians to delight in it – or to learn to do so, for those to whom it does not come naturally.

Poetry however is not merely sing-song rhymes, like the Mother Goose verses. Poetry is a way of expressing truth, a way of knowing what there is to know. When David prays, 'Keep me as the apple of Your eye; Hide me under the shadow of Your wings'[9] we are not to imagine that God, who is a Spirit,[10] has eyes like a man, or wings like a bird (or that David is an apple). Just so, when Jesus says, 'I am the door of the sheep',[11] or 'I am the bread of life'[12] we do not picture Him as made of

---

[9] Psalm 17:8
[10] John 4:24
[11] John 10:7
[12] John 6:35

wood with a doorknob half-way up, or as a fresh-baked loaf of bread, hot from the oven. Such language is poetry, and the Bible is stuffed with it. These images teach us something that a more literal approach cannot. Indeed, it can truly be said that all language is in a sense metaphorical, or symbolic, and therefore, everyone is a poet by virtue of being human. This does not mean, of course, that everyone is a *good* poet. For example, you might say of someone you met, 'he had bright eyes,' which gets to the point, but does not say as much as,

> His eyes would twinkle in his head as bright
> As any star upon a frosty night.[13]

Or, if you were to say, 'his eyes were as bright as Hummer headlights on high-beam,' we may congratulate you on making your point, while critiquing your lack of poetic vision – unless you were aiming at a humorous comparison, which is certainly valid in its place. But beauty of expression, though undervalued in our day, is of prime importance in Scripture, and we would do well to learn from the example of the biblical authors. Listen to this beautiful example of scriptural poetry, and take special note of the various word-pictures David paints:

> Bless the LORD, O my soul…
> And forget not all His benefits…

[13] Geoffrey Chaucer, *The Canterbury Tales*, trans. Nevill Coghill (London: Penguin, 1951), 10.

Who satisfies your mouth with good things,
So that your youth is renewed like the eagle's…
For as the heavens are high above the earth,
So great is His mercy toward those who fear Him;
As far as the east is from the west,
So far has He removed our transgressions from us.
As a father pities his children,
So the LORD pities those who fear Him.
For he knows our frame;
He remembers that we are dust.
As for man, his days are like grass;
As a flower of the field, so he flourishes.
For the wind passes over it, and it is gone,
And its place remembers it no more.[14]

In the Bible, an un-poetic heart does not merely display lack of culture: it reveals a famine of spiritual insight. When Jesus warned the disciples to beware of the 'leaven' of the Pharisees and Sadducees, they thought He was talking about real bread, and Jesus rebuked them for missing the poetic imagery.[15] When Nicodemus came to Jesus by night, our Lord spoke to him of being 'born again'. Nicodemus, completely missing the poetry, asked, 'How can a man be born when he is old?' … 'Are you the teacher of Israel,' asked Jesus, 'and do not know these things?'.[16] In addition, after the Biblical account of Jesus driving

---

[14] Psalm 103:2, 5, 11-16
[15] Matthew 16:5-12
[16] John 3:3, 4, 10. For these insights on Christ's words to his disciples, and to Nicodemus, I am indebted to Dougles Jones, 'Carnal vs. Poetic', *Credenda Agenda*, Volume 13, Issue 5.

the moneychangers from the Temple, we read of another failure of poetic understanding:

> So the Jews answered and said to Him, 'What sign do You show to us, since You do these things?'
> Jesus answered and said to them, 'Destroy this temple, and in three days I will raise it up.'
> Then the Jews said, 'It has taken forty-six years to build this temple, and will You raise it up in three days?'
> But He was speaking of the temple of His body.[17]

The various responses to Jesus's poetic image here are instructive. Years later, when He was on trial, witnesses were brought forward who remembered Jesus's words regarding the Temple. 'We heard Him say, "I will destroy this temple made with hands, and within three days I will build another made without hands"'.[18] The witnesses' account is essentially (though not completely) accurate, and yet the Bible tells us that they bore false witness. How so? Undoubtedly by malicious intent, but certainly part of the problem was blindness to the literal truth behind the poetry. In short, Jesus could have saved Himself a lot of trouble by simply speaking more literally. But the Scriptures tell us that others remembered His words as well: 'Therefore, when He had risen from the dead, His disciples remembered that He had said this to them; and they believed the Scripture and the word which Jesus had said.'[19]

[17] John 2:18-21
[18] Mark 14:58

Despite the disciples' later awakening to His meaning, we are tempted to ask: why does Jesus talk like this? Isn't it better to 'say what you mean', to 'tell it like it is'? If we would be wise, we must pay attention both to what our Lord said and how He chose to say it. The Scriptures as a whole bear witness to the fact that metaphors, similes, vivid word-pictures of every sort, are indispensable when it comes to speaking the truth. One of the main goals of this book is to encourage thoughtful reading of the stories of two men who were masters of incarnating Christian truth in poetic images.

Poetry may be one thing, but what about fairy tales? It is easy enough to suggest that the Bible is full of poetry, and that therefore we have an obligation to read and love poetry, but surely there are no fairy tales in the Scriptures? Isn't that what the sceptics say: that the Bible is no more than oldwives' tales, myths, legends, and fairy tales?

First, it's worth asking – what do we mean by *myth* or *fairy tale*? To most people *myth* usually means *a fictional story*. A nice tale, maybe, but not something that really happened (like the stuff on the news or *Entertainment Tonight*). If this is all the word *myth* may mean, then of course the Bible is *not* mythology. But this limited definition needs challenging. What comes to mind when you hear the word *myth*? Roman, Norse, or Greek stories? Classical tales of the gods? Medieval legends of King Arthur?

[19] John 2:22

What about *fairy tale*? Questing knights, kings, castles, and fair, captive maidens come to mind, but the most memorable characters of fairy tales are often the otherworldly creatures: dragons, unicorns, goblins, elves. For modern minds, these characters mark fairy tales with a deep unreality, thus giving rise to the idea of *fairy tale* as a strictly fictional story, and the common derision of the Bible as 'a bunch of fairy tales'.

Myths and fairy tales however are not *necessarily* fictional. Rather, they embody a particular kind of story – true or imagined – that has a certain inherent literary and emotional power. 'Myth has the ability to make concrete what would otherwise remain abstract,' writes Lewis and Tolkien scholar Colin Duriez. 'In fact, without the shaping of our perception by myth, and other imaginative creations (such as metaphors and models), we would not know real things, only abstractions. There is therefore an intimate connection between myth and thought.'[20] The much-derided 'happy ending', according to Professor J. R. R. Tolkien, is in fact the primary purpose of the fairy tale: 'Far more important is the Consolation of the Happy Ending. Almost I would venture to assert that all complete fairy-stories must have it.'[21]

Tolkien, more than any other writer, has proved that fairy tales still have tremendous power to move and inspire. His greatest work, *The Lord*

---

[20] Colin Duriez, *A Field Guide to Narnia* (Downer's Grove, IL: InterVarsity Press, 2004), 89.
[21] *Poems and Stories*, 175.

of the Rings, was read by more people (over one hundred million) in the twentieth century than any other book, save one: the Bible. Moreover, there is a connection between these two bestsellers: *they are both myths.*

But remember: fairy tales and myths are not necessarily fictional stories. Tolkien described the resurrection of Christ as the happy ending in the greatest of all fairy tales. The resurrection: a fairy tale? Tolkien insists, however, that the Resurrection, though a fairy tale indeed, is not *only* a fairy tale.[22] Think about it this way: God could have (I suppose) secured redemption by providing a mathematical formula for overcoming sin, or abstract philosophical principles to ponder and internalize. Instead, man, by nature a story-teller, would find salvation in the pages of a great and beautiful story.[23]

God is no ordinary author, however, as Tolkien points out. He alone can write a story that is true, not just in the Secondary World of the imagination, but also in Reality. The story of Jesus, then, is *the one Fairy Tale that actually came true*. Try to remember a favourite fairy tale of your childhood (since most adults, for some reason, do not read them), one of particular beauty and power: what if you discovered that it really happened? Such is the reality of Christ's life. The wonder, the hope, and the joy of the Happy Ending are all there, with

[22] See J. R. R. Tolkien, *The Letters of J. R. R. Tolkien*, ed. Humphrey Carpenter (Boston: Houghton Mifflin Company, 1981), 100.
[23] Ibid, 100-101.

one difference: it really happened, in time and space, in the midst of human history.

But will the Bible itself support this fairy tale theory, or is this just the wishful thinking of writers of mythology, imposing their own fancies on the pages of Holy Writ? Let us answer this by remembering the Bible's story.

Adam and Eve ('The Lord Adam and the Lady Eve,' as C. S. Lewis called them in *Prince Caspian*[24]) were the Father and Mother of mankind. They were assailed however by 'the rulers of the darkness of this age' – by 'spiritual hosts of wickedness in the heavenly places',[25] in the form of a serpent.[26]This same crafty being is also known as 'the great dragon'.[27] The Lord and Lady were defeated. But the ancient prophets (are they wizards? – the root word means 'wise'[28]) foretold that a noble prince, the son of the great king, would come and do battle with the dragon.[29] Christ, therefore, in his victory over Satan, is the archetypal dragon-slayer. If that is not enough, we are reminded that the story of redemptive history includes *angels* (Genesis 19; Luke 2:8-15 and Revelation 12:7-9, among many others), *giants* (Numbers 13:32, 33; 1 Samuel 17; 2 Samuel 21:16, 18, 21:20, 22; Job 16:14), *witches* (1 Samuel 28:4-25; 2 Chronicles 33:1, 6; Acts 8:9), *talking animals*

---

[24] C. S. Lewis, *Prince Caspian* (New York: Macmillan Publishing Company, 1951), 211-212.
[25] Ephesians 6:12
[26] Genesis 3:1
[27] Revelation 12:9
[28] See Jeremiah 18:8, Daniel 2:21, 48
[29] Genesis 3:15, Isaiah 7:14, Micah 5:2

(Genesis 3:1-6; Numbers 2:21-33; 2 Peter 2:14-16) and even *unicorns* (Numbers 23:22; 24:8; Deuteronomy 33:17; Job 39:9; Psalm 22:21; 29:6; 92:10; Isaiah 34:7[30]). Pastor and writer Douglas Wilson observes that, in fact, 'the gospel can be presented in scriptural language, and yet sound an awful lot like a fairy tale. Moreover, it is an interesting fairy tale. This does not make Scripture false – rather, it makes traditional fairy stories truer than we have assumed.'[31]

Because the statements made above will sound so strange to many readers, I must take just a moment at this point to say clearly what I do and do not mean. Again, if a fairy tale is no more than a fictional story, then I will be the loudest in proclaiming that the story of Christ is not a fairy tale. If myths may never be true, then the Bible is not a myth. Perhaps it will be helpful if we say *the story of Christ and of God's work in human history has all the elements of a good fairy tale*: kings and princes, dragons and serpents, dangers and epic battles, talking beasts and otherworldly

---

[30] Most modern translations will use the word "ox", but with little or no textual warrant. Doug Wilson explains: "All these passages are translating the word *re'em*, for which no modern lexicographer knows (directly) the meaning. But the ancient translators of the Septuagint, centuries before Christ, translated them all with the Greek word *monoceros*. The Latin transliteration of this is *unicorn*." (Douglas Wilson, "Love Story," *Credenda Agenda*, Volume 15, Issue 6). Though I have added my own observations, I am indebted to this article by Douglas Wilson for some of the insights contained in this paragraph.

[31] Douglas Wilson, "Love Story," *Credenda Agenda*, Volume 15, Issue 6.

creatures, miracles and joy (the happy ending). But because it is so important, I will say again that if it is indeed a fairy tale, then *it is the one fairy tale that came true.*

Tolkien's friend, C. S. Lewis, author of the beloved fairy tales known to the world as *The Chronicles of Narnia*, described the Christian story in similar terms. 'The heart of Christianity is a myth which is also a fact,' Lewis said. 'The old myth of the dying god, *without ceasing to be myth*, comes down from the heaven of legend and imagination to the earth of history. It *happens* – at a particular date, in a particular place, followed by definable historical consequences.'[32]

We must consistently emphasise both *myth and history* as we teach God's Word to our children. That is, we do not sacrifice either the wonder, the miraculous joy on the one hand, or the solid truth of history on the other. As Tolkien put it, 'Legend and History have met and fused.'[33] I once heard of a student who said the one phrase in the Apostle's Creed he could never bring himself to say was 'under Pontius Pilate' ('He suffered under Pontius Pilate'), because that put a historical date on it. He could believe in a nice moral fable, an inspiring parable, but the problem was, Christians always insisted that the thing actually happened. Let us remember, then, that the story of Christ

---

[32] C. S. Lewis, "Myth Became Fact," *The Grand Miracle and Other Selected Essays on Theology and Ethics from God in the Dock*, ed. Walter Hooper (New York: Ballantine Books, 1970), 41.
[33] *Poems and Stories*, 180.

begins, not with 'Once upon a time' – or the contemporary counterpart, 'Long, long ago, in a galaxy far, far away' – but with, 'In the days of Herod, king of Judea....'

If we understand the Bible as a single, unified story, with Christ as the central character, we will begin to see it, not as 'Neat Tips for Living,' but as the great Divine Drama, the most exciting tale ever written. As we battle the dominant culture to impress upon our children the centrality of Christ, the forgiveness of sins, and all that is encompassed within the Christian message, we have one great weapon to wield: the Story itself. Those who think of the Bible as nothing more than theological propositions on the one hand or a how-to manual on the other, should remember the words of Dorothy L. Sayers: 'The Christian faith is the greatest drama that ever staggered the imagination of man – and the dogma [doctrine] is the drama.'[34] Christianity has doctrine, to be sure, but it is revealed to us primarily through the moving, exciting, dramatic, sorrowful, joyful, *true* stories of Scripture – in letters, poetry, history, dreams, visions, and… fairy tales.

Sayers, a contemporary and acquaintance of Lewis and Tolkien, was amazed that Christians had managed to make their doctrine boring. She believed this was because most did not know the Story as well as they thought. 'If this is dull, then what, in Heaven's name, is worthy to be called

---

[34] Dorothy L. Sayers, *Creed or Chaos?* (Manchester, NH, Sophia Institute Press, 1949), 3.

exciting?'[35] You really have to work to make *this* tale boring. The account of God becoming man, and being murdered by man, only to conquer death itself to save man, may be shocking, but never dull. Tell *that* story to the world and, according to Sayers, 'they may not believe it; but at least they may realize that here is something that a man may be glad to believe.'[36]

'Let us, in Heaven's name,' wrote Sayers, 'drag out the Divine Drama from under the dreadful accumulation of slipshod thinking and trashy sentiment heaped upon it, and set it on an open stage to startle the world into some sort of vigorous reaction.'[37] It is interesting to note that Sayers, a playwright, referred to the story of Christ as 'the Divine Drama', while Tolkien and Lewis, writers of myths and fairy tales, used phrases like 'the greatest Fairy Story' or 'a myth which is also a fact'. The common thread, however, is story. This is what we need, then: a new generation of storytellers – parents, teachers, pastors – who understand the Bible as both myth and history, and who will tell, with passion and wonder, the greatest Fairy Tale ever written. We must pass on the great chronicles of the Divine Drama, without altering the script. The image is one of children sitting around a fire at night, while their elders recount the breathtaking tales of days gone by, recapturing the imaginations of the young with

[35] Ibid, 6.
[36] Ibid, 25.
[37] Ibid, 24.

the true myth, the fairy tale that came true… once upon a time, in the days of Herod, King of Judea.

Family Activities

1. Get the family together and read through the Scriptures mentioned in this chapter. Ask everyone for his or her thoughts. How do these passages, considered together, affect the way you view the Bible? Do you accept these as accurate historical accounts, or do you find yourself embarrassed, wishing you could explain such fantastic passages away? What would your unbelieving friends or family think of you if they knew you believed such things? Discuss your thoughts with your family and pray for grace never to be embarrassed by any part of God's Word.

2. Find a good collection of fairy tales (if you don't already have one) and begin reading through them at night as a family. Look for common themes and patterns. Do these themes and patterns remind you of what Tolkien called the greatest fairy story – the story of Christ? In what ways? Discuss the similarities or differences with your children.

3. Read through one of the four Gospels as a family. Whenever an Old Testament passage is quoted, look it up, and read it as well. Begin to see the story of Christ as the climax of the Bible's one story, and begin training your family to see the Bible in two ways: first, as the unified account

35

of God's work in history and the salvation of His people (and thus as much more than a Collection of Practical Tips or a Handbook of Answers For Improving Your Life); and second, as your own family history.

4. Read through the Psalms and look for the poetic imagery used (do this when reading any portion of Scripture). Some examples would include metaphors (as when John calls Jesus 'the Lamb of God') or similes (as when the Psalmist writes in Psalm 1:3 that the man who delights in the Law of the Lord is 'like a tree planted by the rivers of water, that brings forth its fruit in its season, whose leaf also shall not wither'. Similes are usually preceded by 'like' or 'as'). Discuss what the writer is trying to convey by using such imagery. Practise, with your family, coming up with such word-pictures to describe things, people, or situations.

CHAPTER TWO ⊕

J.R.R. TOLKIEN AND C.S. LEWIS:
A CREATIVE FRIENDSHIP

...We owed each a great debt to the other, and that tie, with the deep affection that it begot, remains. He was a great man...[38]

J. R. R. tolkien, after the death of
C. S. Lewis

*Tolkien...is most important. **The Hobbit** is merely the adaptation to children of part of a huge private mythology of a most serious kind: the whole cosmic struggle as he sees it but mediated through an imaginary world...This is the private world of a Christian. He is a very great man.*[39]

C. S. LEWIS

---

[38] Quoted in C. S. Lewis, *The Grand Miracle and Other Selected Essays on Theology and Ethics from God in the Dock*, ed. Walter Hooper (New York: Ballantine Books, 1970).

[39] C. S. Lewis, *Letters of C. S. Lewis*, ed. W. H. Lewis (San Diego: Harcourt, Inc., 1966, 1988), 376.

*t*he snow falls heavily and persistently outside, but inside, the electric fire is roaring, banishing the cold air to much-deserved exile. Inside the room, gathered around the jolly hearth, some half a dozen men are sitting, cups of tea in their hands, talking together on this wintry Thursday evening in Oxford, England. The smoke from several pipes lends a pleasing aroma and a fitting mood to the assembly. They gather here most Thursdays in the college rooms of a man known to his friends as Jack. The meetings are informal: no predetermined agenda takes up their time. These men get together each week to read to each other, and to talk about what they have read.

As the laughter fades after the telling of a joke, Jack sets his tea on a small table, glancing at one of his companions, who, at the moment, is refilling his pipe.

'Well, has nobody got anything to read us?' Three or four of the men begin to bring out papers, and Jack chuckles. 'Very well, but we can't all read at once. I understand Tollers has a treat tonight, and one that I am particularly looking forward to – the first chapter of the new Hobbit book.'

A few raised eyebrows in otherwise stolid faces are the only reaction to the announcement: some of those present are less eager than others for more stories of hobbits from 'Tollers', also known as Professor J.R.R. Tolkien. But Jack – professionally known as C. S. Lewis – had enthusiastically reviewed *The Hobbit* upon its publication for the *Times*

Literary Supplement in London. *'The Hobbit,'* he had written, 'may well prove a classic.'[40]

Tollers rises, blows a final puff of smoke, and sets the pipe on the mantel. He picks up a handwritten manuscript, returns to his chair, clears his throat, and begins to read:

> *'When Bilbo, son of Bungo of the family of Baggins, prepared to celebrate his seventieth birthday there was for a day or two some talk in the neighbourhood.'[41]*

Think of the friendships in your life. What was it that first drew you together? Was it merely the desire for a friend, or was there a common interest that sparked the friendship? Every friendship is different, with its own unique joys and loves: sports, reading, movies, music, or poetry are but a few examples. These interests forge a common bond, and help hold the friendship together.

In Oxford, England, beginning in the 1930s, there was a group of friends that gathered once or

---

[40] Quoted in Colin Duriez, *Tolkien and C. S. Lewis: The Gift of Friendship* (Mahwah, NJ: HiddenSpring, 2003), 90.

[41] J. R. R. Tolkien, *The Return of The Shadow: The History of the Lord of the Rings, Part One* (Boston: Houghton Mifflin Company, 1988), 13.

twice a week. Like all such gatherings, they had their common interests. One of the friends in this little group described their common bond as 'a tendency to write, and Christianity'.[42] Not that this little circle of companions never talked of anything but their writings and their faith, but these things were central, and held them together for many years. Some groups of friends gather so regularly, and so often, they become a sort of club – and as clubs generally have names, this one called itself the Inklings. The name had been inherited from an earlier version of the group, and referred to the fact that the members were writers (it may be hard to remember this in the age of computers, but writers once actually *wrote*: with pen and *ink* – thus the name, the '*Ink*lings').

The Inklings are important to us because the two most well known members were none other than C. S. Lewis and J.R.R. Tolkien. Writer Colin Duriez remarks that, 'Tolkien was undoubtedly a central figure in this literary group of friends, though it was held together by Lewis's zest and enthusiasm.'[43] In these friendly meetings, some of the best-loved books of the last hundred years were first read aloud. Lewis described one of the meetings of the Inklings this way:'On Thursday we had a meeting of the Inklings…The bill of fare afterwards consisted of a section of the new Hobbit book from Tolkien, a nativity play from Williams… and a chapter out of the book on the

---

[42] Quoted in *Tolkien and C. S. Lewis*, 86.
[43] Ibid, 79.

Problem of Pain from me.'[44] 'Williams' refers to Charles Williams, novelist and playwright, and a key member of the Inklings for a number of years. 'The new Hobbit book' refers, of course, to *The Lord of the Rings*.

The Inklings gathered in several different locations over the years, but most often they met on Tuesday mornings at The Eagle and Child pub (which they usually called 'The Bird and Baby') and on Thursday evenings in C. S. Lewis's rooms at Magdalen College in Oxford, where he was a tutor. These Thursday meetings were the main time for each member to read their latest chapter, poem, or essay to the other Inklings. All enjoyed these readings, but Tolkien remembered that Lewis especially loved hearing others read their work, and possessed a remarkable memory of what he heard.[45]

Imagine, if you will, that you have written a poem or story, painted a picture, composed a song, or otherwise created something with your own hands – something that was your own idea. Perhaps, like many people, you found yourself at least a little shy about showing it to others when it was done. Maybe you thought they would not like it, or understand it; maybe you were worried it was not that good. Now imagine that you and your friends have formed a club where the only

---

[44] C. S. Lewis, *Letters of C. S. Lewis*, ed. W. H. Lewis (San Diego: Harcourt, Inc., 1966, 1988), 328.
[45] See J. R. R. Tolkien, *The Letters of J. R. R. Tolkien*, ed. Humphrey Carpenter (Boston: Houghton Mifflin Company, 1981), 388.

rules are that you must bring, to each meeting, the poem,story, picture or song; you must read or show it to the other members of the club; and you must let them tell you exactly what they think of it. Suppose also that your friends are completely honest, and unafraid to speak their minds. If you can imagine what that might be like, you will have a good idea of what the Inklings meetings were all about. 'To read to the Inklings was a formidable ordeal,' wrote W. H. Lewis, C. S. Lewis's brother, and himself a member of the Inklings, 'and I can still remember the fear with which I offered the first chapter of my first book – and my delight, too, at its reception.'[46] Not only did the other members listen to the latest chapter of *The Lord of the Rings*, or Lewis's science fiction trilogy, but they discussed what they had heard – whether they liked it or not. They were generous in their praise, and their criticism, openly speaking their minds on both the strengths and weaknesses of each other's work. Lewis spoke of this honest criticism, remembering that Charles Williams's *All Hallow's Eve*, his *Perelandra* (the second volume of the Space Trilogy), and Tolkien's *The Lord of the Rings* were all read in serial installments, chapter by chapter, and that many of the strengths of those books came from the no-holds-barred critical commentary of the Inklings.[47] The criticism was

[46] C. S. Lewis, *Letters of C. S. Lewis*, ed. W. H. Lewis (San Diego: Harcourt, Inc., 1966, 1988), 34.
[47] See Colin Duriez and David Porter, *The Inklings Handbook: The*

honest and straightforward, even when it involved a negative opinion. After hearing a difficult section of Charles Williams's writings at a meeting of the Inklings, Lewis (who loved Williams and his work) exclaimed, 'Charles, you're impossible.'[48] This was characteristic of Lewis; Tolkien, praising Lewis's unyielding honesty, once indicated that not even friendship would induce Jack to say anything but what he meant.[49]

Friendship was important to Lewis, who wrote on the subject in his book *The Four Loves*. In that book, friendship is presented as one of the four main kinds of love humans can have for each other. Lewis believed that modern people do not understand friendship as well as they once did. Yet good friendships are among the sweetest of God's blessings. 'Life,' he wrote of friendship in *The Four Loves*, 'has no better gift to give. Who could have deserved it?'[50]

The Inklings were Lewis's friends, and Tolkien was certainly among the best. Though they did not always see eye to eye, they had a number of things in common – which is, of course necessary for a friendship to begin in the first place. For Lewis, friendships are formed around a common interest. Perhaps you have had a similar experience: that

Lives, Thought and Writings of C. S. Lewis, J. R. R. Tolkien, Charles Williams, Owen Barfield and Their Friends (St Louis: Chalice Press, 2001), 4.
[48] Quoted in *Tolkien and C. S. Lewis*, 119.
[49] See *The Letters* of *J. R. R. Tolkien*, 23.
[50] C. S. Lewis, *The Beloved Works of C. S. Lewis* (Edison, NJ: Inspirational Press, 2004), 252.

moment when you realize the other person shares your love of a certain kind of music, a favourite book, or a particular game or sport. And at that moment, as Lewis describes it, you exclaim, 'What? You too? I thought I was the only one.'[51] Friendships are born in such moments. Lewis and Tolkien became friends after just such a moment. Tolkien later wrote that his friendship with Lewis was forged from similar tastes, and a common interest in books.[52]

Friendship, then, needs not only at least two people, but also a third thing – the music, the sport or the book. According to Lewis, friendships are always about *something*, even if that something is no more than 'an enthusiasm for dominoes or white mice'.[53] Friends need the common interest that brings them together, and mostly spend their time talking about or enjoying what they both love. The image Lewis paints is of two friends, side by side, looking, not at each other, but at the common interest. Of course, friendship can be and often is deeper than this: true friends care about each other as well, helping when times of need arise. But it begins with the common love.

We can see this sort of friendship in the writings of both Lewis and Tolkien. For example, in *The Last Battle*, from Lewis's *The Chronicles of Narnia*, King Tirian of Narnia meets seven people from our world who call themselves 'the seven friends

---

[51] Ibid., 248.
[52] See *The Letters of J. R. R. Tolkien*, 23.
[53] *The Beloved Works of C. S. Lewis*, 249.

of Narnia'.[54] 'Friends' here may be understood in two ways. First, as friends *of* Narnia, they are friends *to* Narnia – that is, they are loyal allies of Narnia's land and people. But second, the seven friends are also friends to each other – friends who have been bound together by their common love of Narnia, and their common experience as being among those happy few from our world who had been to Narnia. Here, Narnia is the common bond that forged the friendship. Moreover, in *The Lord of the Rings*, a strong friendship forms between perhaps the two most unlikely people: Legolas the Elf and Gimli the Dwarf. If you know the story, you are aware that Elves and Dwarves were, at best, deeply distrustful of each other. Yet Gimli and Legolas became friends, bound together, in this case, by a common cause: the Quest of the Ring-bearer and the part played in that Quest by the Fellowship of the Ring, of which both were a part.

Lewis, Tolkien, and the other Inklings shared common interests as well. As Lewis mentioned, they were all writers, and they were all Christians, or interested in Christianity. Tolkien's Christian faith, shared with his friend Lewis, gave them a profound unity, though in some ways, it also kept them at a distance from one another, especially in their later years (Tolkien, a Roman Catholic, never quite came to terms with the fact

---

[54] C. S. Lewis, *The Last Battle* (New York: Macmillan Publishing Company, 1956), 43.

that Lewis remained a Protestant). The friendship, however, deeply impacted the men as writers, as both admitted. Praising Lewis's generosity and friendship, Tolkien wrote that the great debt he owed Lewis was the encouragement he offered Tolkien during the long years of writing his stories. It was only Lewis, Tolkien would note, that gave him the idea that the 'legendarium' of Middle-earth (including *The Silmarillion* and *The Lord of the Rings*) could ever be more than a personal diversion. Indeed, Tolkien believed that *The Lord of the Rings*, in particular, would never have seen print apart from Lewis.[55] Lewis encouraged Tolkien as a writer, however, precisely because Tolkien's labours in the invention of Middle-earth had greatly encouraged Lewis. As he put it, *The Lord of the Rings*, 'is the book we have all been waiting for'.[56] Tolkien's mythology influenced Lewis's writing so much that bits and pieces of the Middle-earth legendarium found their way into Lewis's stories. As an example, Lewis referred to 'Numinor' and 'the True West' in *That Hideous Strength*, the third volume of his Ransom science-fiction trilogy. Lewis himself explained the origin of these allusions: 'Those who would like to learn further about Numinor and the True West must (alas!) await the publication of much that still exists only in the MSS. [manuscripts] of my friend, Professor J. R. R. Tolkien.'[57]

---

[55] See *The Letters of J. R. R. Tolkien*, 362.
[56] *Letters of C. S. Lewis*, 458.

But why such an emphasis on this notable literary friendship? One of the themes of this book is that storytelling is inevitably at its best when it is the product of community, of covenantal relationships. The children's books of Tolkien, as we shall see, invariably sprang from stories he had invented to comfort or entertain his children. In addition, the fiction of both Tolkien and Lewis was forged in the delightful, honest, critical friendship between these two men. The best art is always the product of community, and history bears this out. 'Historically, the greatest periods of creativity have been the result of community,'[58] writes musician and Biblical scholar Michael Card. Card goes on to contrast the great artistic 'schools' (such as that of Verrocchio, where Leonardo da Vinci was tutored) with the modern ideal of the lone artist, struggling for acceptance in the absence of constructive criticism, apprenticeship, and artistic accountability. Such artistic values, he notes, are discouraged in the modern artistic milieu for two reasons. 'First, the commercial system is based on individualism (celebrityism). Second, production schedules rarely afford the time required for someone to be nurtured in

---

[57] C. S. Lewis, *That Hideous Strength: A Modern Fairy-Tale for Grown-Ups* (New York: Macmillan Publishing Co., Inc., 1946), 7, cf. *The Letters of J. R. R. Tolkien*, 303. Lewis had heard Tolkien's word "Numenor" read aloud as part of *The Silmarillion* and *The Lord of the Rings*, but did not know the precise spelling.

[58] Michael Card, *Scribbling in the Sand: Christ and Creativity* (Downer's Grove, IL: InterVarsity Press, 2002), 107.

his or her craft. In the absence of community, the artist experiences a sense of aloneness and defeat.'[59]

As Card demonstrates, this sense of art in community is also a biblical priority. As Christians, and as parents, we should strive to impart a sense of community to our children, whether in our Christian beliefs, or in the artistic values we pass on to them. Even those who may believe they have no 'creative talents' (though creativity takes many more forms than just the usual artistic expressions) can benefit from a community-centred approach to art. Whether or not we are artists ourselves, we are responsible for passing on great art (of whatever sort) to our children. If we do not teach them to love great stories, beautiful music, inspiring poetry, and even good films, we can be sure that the unbelieving culture around us will rush to fill the void with its own offerings.

The friendship and writings of Lewis and Tolkien, therefore, serve us in two ways: they embody the ideal of good storytelling as a result of community relationships; and, for those looking for the best stories to read to their children at night, the magnificent books of these two friends are just about the best place to start.

---

[59] Ibid., 112.

Family Activities

1. Regularly schedule creative times with your family. This would be an afternoon, perhaps, in which everyone gets together and works on various creative endeavours. Each person can work on an individual project, or, if everyone is interested, you could have a family project. If you are already aware of some of the creative interests of your children, this will be a way to encourage them to develop that interest. If not, this will be a good time to begin to discover talents and desires. One may write a short story, or poem; another may play a song on the violin, piano, flute, guitar, or other instrument. One may paint a picture; another may perform a dramatic recitation of lines from a play or favourite book. When everyone is finished, discuss the various works together. Offer generous praise, but also constructive criticism. Find out whether each work was enjoyed. Perhaps one child will find out that painting is not his thing, though he decides he would like to try to write a poem like his sister (and please let's have none of this nonsense about poetry being only for girls – read *Beowulf* or *Sir Gawain and the Green Knight* and you'll never think that again). If Mom or Dad have abilities in a particular creative area, and one or more of the children desire to learn their art, this is a great opportunity for genuine, covenantal and artistic apprenticeship, so don't miss it.

2. Dad and Mom: take time to discuss with each other the kind of stories (or other art) that you want to pass on to your children. Keep Philippians 4:8 in mind as you do this: 'Finally, brethren, whatever things are true, whatever things are noble, whatever things are just, whatever things are pure, whatever things are lovely, whatever things are of good report, if there is any virtue and if there is anything praiseworthy – meditate on these things.' Let this Scripture be a theme verse for your family, especially as you enjoy books, music, movies, art, and similar. Take the time to educate yourself about culture and the way it affects our lives. An excellent book to get you started in this is, *All God's Children and Blue Suede Shoes: Christians and Popular Culture* by Ken Myers. Discuss the book together, and determine to fill your family's lives with truth, goodness, and beauty. Go out of your way to find stories that embody these noble virtues, and spend time telling these stories to your children. Spiritually healthy children should always be clamouring for more stories, and parents should delight in this, for good stories are an important part of the process of building character.

CHAPTER THREE

WORD AND IMAGE: THE
STORYTELLING OF TOLKIEN AND LEWIS

And I don't believe anyone knows exactly how he 'makes things up'. Making up is a very mysterious thing. When you 'have an idea' could you tell anyone exactly how you thought of it?[60]

C. S. LEWIS

FOR all their points in common, Lewis and Tolkien were very different in many ways. One difference was in their approach to writing stories: they began their tale-spinning in very different (almost opposite) ways. Tolkien was a philologist ('lover of words' – his academic work involved the study of the development of languages); indeed, some would say the leading philologist of his day, a linguistic expert unmatched

---

[60] C. S. Lewis, "It All Began With A Picture..." *Of Other Worlds: Essays and Stories*, ed. Walter Hooper (San Diego: Harcourt Brace and Company, 1966), 42.

in breadth of knowledge, and depth of insight.[61] Accordingly, he generally began his stories with words and names, particularly with his own invented languages. As he put it, 'a name comes first and the story follows'.[62] So deep was his love and knowledge of his subject that Lewis once said of him, 'He had been inside language.'[63]

For those who may not have understood the reference to invented languages, a little more of the story is necessary. Tolkien's love of languages did not merely extend to the study of existent tongues, but to the invention of new ones. 'Real' (existent) languages were often the inspiration for these invented languages (*Quenya*, or 'High-elven' has its roots in Latin, Greek, and Finnish, while *Sindarin*, or 'Grey-elven', is based on British-Welsh[64]). Just as real speech and dialect change over time, so Tolkien incorporated gradual modifications, a sort of linguistic history, to his languages, mirroring the way real language develops in a culture throughout centuries of use and change. These languages required stories, peoples, and histories, to give them life. Tolkien breathed life into his languages by creating the world and peoples of Middle-earth: hobbits, elves, dwarves, ents, orcs, and men.

---

[61] For an excellent treatment of Tolkien's philological gifts and work, see the first two chapters of Tom Shippey's important work, *The Road to Middle-Earth: How J. R. R. Tolkien Created a New Mythology*.

[62] J. R. R. Tolkien, *The Letters of J. R. R. Tolkien*, ed. Humphrey Carpenter (Boston: Houghton Mifflin Company, 1981), 219.

[63] Quoted in Humphrey Carpenter, *J. R. R. Tolkien: A Biography* (Boston: Houghton Mifflin Company, 2000), 144.

[64] See *The Letters of J. R. R. Tolkien*, 176.

One example of Tolkien's pattern of 'names first, stories after' is found in the development of *The Hobbit*, one of his best-loved stories. While engaged in the wearisome task of marking examination papers, Tolkien, finding to his joy a blank page among the papers, suddenly wrote on the sheet the words that would eventually become the opening sentence of *The Hobbit*: 'In a hole in the ground there lived a hobbit.' He did not then know why, or where the sentence had come from, but eventually he decided to find out, and the result was the story of Bilbo Baggins[65] (see Chapter 8 of this book for a discussion of *The Hobbit*).

C. S. Lewis took a different approach to writing his stories. In his short essay, 'It All Began With A Picture,' Lewis reveals that both the Narnian Chronicles, and his science-fiction trilogy, 'began with seeing pictures in my head. At first they were not a story, just pictures.'[66] In the case of *The Lion, the Witch and the Wardrobe*, the picture was one he had had in his head since the age of sixteen: a faun[67] walking through a snowy wood, carrying an umbrella and parcels. About a quarter of a century later, he decided to write a story about the picture.

---

[65] Ibid, p. 215.

[66] *Of Other Worlds*, 42.

[67] The "fauni" were half-men, half-goat creatures that Lewis borrowed from Greek and Roman mythology (see Arthur Cotterell and Rachel Storm, *The Ultimate Encyclopedia of Mythology* [London: Hermes House, 2003], 44).

Later, while writing the story, as he describes it, 'Aslan came bounding into it.'[68] (For those of you new to the books, Aslan is the great Lion, the Son of the Emperor Over the Sea, and the Christ-figure in the Narnian books. We will meet him later, in Chapter 12.) The entrance of Aslan came about in much the same way the Faun's had earlier: with a picture, for Lewis had been dreaming about lions a lot at the time.[69]

Lewis described the early process of writing a story as somewhat like 'bird-watching',[70] in which he would begin to see more and more pictures that seemed to go together. He theorised that it might be possible for a whole set of mental pictures to form such a consistent whole that an entire story would emerge, without the author actually having to write it. He added, however, that he himself had never been that lucky. Instead, there were always 'gaps', and here is where the writer in Lewis would take over, inventing and crafting a story around the pictures. The process was one of trying to decide what the people or creatures in the picture might be doing. 'I have no idea,' he wrote, 'whether this is the usual way of writing stories, still less whether it is the best. It is the only one I know: images always come first.'[71]

So, for Tolkien: 'a name comes first and the story follows'. And for Lewis: 'images always

---

[68] *Of Other Worlds*, 42.
[69] Ibid.
[70] "On Three Ways of Writing for Children," in *Of Other Worlds* 32.
[71] *Of Other Worlds*, 33.

come first'. Two quite different approaches, and yet both have been wildly successful. Since success is not always the best test of worth, however, perhaps we can ask whether either approach is preferable? Does either method yield better stories? Or is one more in keeping with a Christian worldview than the other? The last question may seem to some strange or pointless – after all, what can questions of storytelling method have to do with faith in Christ? – and yet, it seems to me, we can find an answer to this question, in the unlikely source of Holy Scripture itself.

God, as we have already discussed, is the great storyteller of history. As he writes the story of His people (and of everyone else) it is worth noticing the methods He uses – in particular, in the crowning moment of the story, the life of Jesus Christ, which Tolkien, as we have noted, described as the greatest happy ending in the greatest fairy story. How, then, does God tell the true story of Christ: by Tolkien's method of the Word, or Lewis's of the Image?

Let us begin by looking at the first chapter of John's Gospel: 'In the beginning was the Word, and the Word was with God, and the Word was God.' Christ Himself, in the inspired pages of the Bible, is described as the Word. We are told that 'the Word became flesh and dwelt among us, and we beheld His glory. ...' Christ is the *eternal* Logos, or Word, which would indicate that the Word came first (being eternal) and the story (at least in its incarnate form) after. This, as we have seen, is Tolkien's method.

So, is the question answered? Is Tolkien's way superior, divinely blessed and endorsed? Perhaps, but there is one more passage to examine. In Colossians 1:15, St Paul writes of Christ: 'He is the *image* of the invisible God, the firstborn over all creation' (emphasis added). Here, Christ is the *icon*, the image of the invisible God, which is another way of saying, 'the Word became flesh' – truly God (invisible), truly man (visible). 'He who has seen Me has seen the Father,' Jesus says.[72]

Jesus Christ is the Word of God. Jesus Christ is the Image of the invisible God. Word and Image. Tolkien and Lewis. But God is a better storyteller than these gifted men. He is not limited to this or that method – He crafts His tale, not on paper only, but through a Word that lives, and an Image that is also a Word. Moreover, He writes His story, not on the pages of history, but in history itself; not in what Tolkien called the Secondary World of the imagination, but in the Primary World – history, time, space, matter, reality. We may imitate His creativeness in our own stories and books, but we cannot duplicate what the only-wise God has created. Let us marvel anew at the riches of His story, in the pages of Scripture, history, and in our own lives.

---

[72] John 14:9

FAMILY ACTIVITIES

1. As you read books and stories, especially the Bible, keep an eye out for unfamiliar words or phrases. Make a point of looking them up in a good dictionary. Ask yourselves why the author chose to use certain words at certain points. Learn to get more out of reading by learning new words. Practise using new words. Have family times in which a new word is learned, and everyone, together, makes up a story, using only that word (or perhaps three or four new words) as a beginning. Begin to see language and words as a gift of God, a way to understand more about Him, and each other, and a way to express thanksgiving and praise to Him.

2. Practise 'seeing pictures' like Lewis. This of course is just another way of saying, 'use your imagination'. In fact, 'man is so made,' wrote Lewis's friend Dorothy L. Sayers, 'that he has no way to think except in pictures.'[73] But some think more vividly in this respect than others. Have another family time in which everyone tells of a dream they have had, or an image that has come to mind; they can even try to picture something then and there. As with words in your earlier family time, try to make up a story around the pictures (write down the various picture-ideas on paper, and try to connect them in a story). Like

---

[73] Dorothy L. Sayers, *The Mind of the Maker* (San Francisco: Harper Collins, 1979), 22.

Lewis, fill in the gaps between the pictures with your own ideas of what is happening in the story. Talk to your children about the Bible's declaration that Christ is the 'image of the invisible God'. Read John 1:14, 18. Discuss with them what it means that God, invisible in Himself, became visible in the incarnation of Christ. What does that mean for us, as human beings made in the image of God? Is there comfort or encouragement in this aspect of God's story?

CHAPTER FOUR

STARTING AT HOME: THE CHILDREN'S WRITINGS OF J. R. R. TOLKIEN

It is true that the age of childhood-sentiment has produced some delightful books (especially charming, however, to adults) of the fairy kind or near to it; but it has also produced a dreadful undergrowth of stories written or adapted to what was or is conceived to be the measure of children's minds and needs.[74]

J. R. R. tolkien

It seems strange to imagine, but the very idea of children's books is a recent historical invention. The late Kathryn Lindskoog, who wrote many books on the writings of C. S. Lewis, notes that, for most of history, 'there was no such thing as a children's book. There were no children's writers

---

[74] J. R. R. Tolkien, "On Fairy-Stories," in *Tree and Leaf: Including the Poem Mythopoeia, The Homecoming of Beorhtnoth* (London: Harper Collins Publishers, 2001), 43.

at all. People told stories to children, but no one wrote a storybook for them to enjoy until 250 years ago. Books for children came along like an afterthought in the book world.'[75]

There has not always been a market for such books, and for a very good reason: storytelling was once primarily the domain of the family. Fathers and mothers told stories to their children, who in turn told them to their children. Stories were a major part of the culture that was passed down from generation to generation.

This notion of a storytelling culture, handed down from father to son, from mother to daughter, may seem strange to those of us raised in the modern world. After all, our diversions and amusements come packaged according to highly specific demographic categories: Dad reads his mystery thriller, Mom her paperback romance, brother his *Harry Potter*, and sister her *Sweet Valley High* book. Each member of the family has his or her own music, movies, clothing styles, magazines, schedule, and life. We are no longer families, with unique family identities; we are merely loosely connected groups of individuals who happen to live under the same roof.[76]

It was not always so. Families once read together, enjoying the same stories, songs, and

---

[75] Kathryn Lindskoog, *Journey Into Narnia* (Pasadena, California: Hope Publishing House, 1998), ix.

[76] The substance of this illustration is from R. C. Sproul, Jr, ed., *Family Practice: God's Prescription for a Healthy Home* (Phillipsburgh, NJ: P & R Publishing, 2001), 3.

foods. They were themselves a part of a larger culture that supported them in this, but each family was itself a little culture, developing its own traditions, rituals, and memories. Today, Mom and Dad have no stories that were handed down to them (except maybe their memories of Disney films), and so they have nothing to pass on to their little ones. Today, many children's books are written by specialists, who may or may not have children of their own. Child psychologists write books that are the product of much research, ensuring that each reader will have age-appropriate storylines, themes, characters, and vocabularies.[77] Never mind that the stories are often as thin as the paper they are printed on: the scientific age has declared its findings, and one discovery is that parents are no longer capable, apart from professional assistance, of telling stories to their children.

One of the goals of this book is to encourage a culture of storytelling in families, and a good way to do this is by highlighting those authors who wrote, not only for 'children' as a class, but for specific children, whose names and faces the author knew (usually because they belonged to

---

[77] The famous Dr Seuss was forced to write, on one occasion, from a list of 223 pre-selected words, a 'controlled vocabulary' for children, supplied by his publisher. Though from it he was able to write *The Cat in the Hat*, he 'decided later that controlled vocabulary was a poor idea.' (See Kathryn Lindskoog and Ranelda Mack Hunsicker, *How to Grow a Young Reader: Books from Every Age for Readers of Every Age* [Colorado Springs: Shaw Books, 1999, 2002], 32.)

his or her own children). This was once more common than now. A. A. Milne wrote his famous Pooh stories for his son, Christopher Robin. George MacDonald, the nineteenth-century Scottish novelist and fairy-tale writer, read to his children, and his stories, in addition to their wider publication, were handed down through his family as well. His granddaughter remembered, 'My love for my grandfather's Fairy Tales was started at an early age – about five, I think – because my father (Bernard MacDonald) read them to me at night as bedtime stories. As I grew older, the children's books ... became very familiar to me and my small friends.'[78]

One of the best examples of a children's writer who wrote primarily for his own children is none other than J. R. R. Tolkien. All of Tolkien's published children's writings were, in their origin, stories he made up for his own children. Indeed, several were not published until after his death, when demand for his writings had increased dramatically. Tolkien made up stories for his children in a variety of situations. When his eldest son, John, could not sleep, he told him stories about Carrots, 'a boy with red hair who climbed into a cuckoo clock and went off on a series of strange adventures'.[79] Every year, as Christmas neared, he would compose

---

[78] George MacDonald, *The Gifts of the Child Christ & Other Stories and Fairy Tales*, ed. Glenn Edward Sadler (Grand Rapids, Michigan: William B. Eerdmans Publishing Company, 1973, 1996), vi.

[79] Humphrey Carpenter, *J. R. R. Tolkien: A Biography* (Boston: Houghton Mifflin Company, 2000), 164.

a letter from Father Christmas, addressed to the Tolkien children. These letters were posthumously collected and published as *The Father Christmas Letters*. The Tolkien family's purchase of their first automobile sparked the tale of *Mr Bliss*, who has a series of misadventures related to his car. When his son, Michael, lost a favourite toy dog on the beach, Tolkien spun a tale about just such a dog who, having been turned into a toy by a wizard, is lost by a little boy on a beach, and then embarks on a variety of adventures on the moon and under the sea. This story was published in 1998, twenty-five years after Tolkien's death, as *Roverandom*. And of course, the most famous of Tolkien's children's books is the story of Bilbo Baggins, and his adventure recapturing the treasure of the Dwarves from Smaug, the Dragon – a story known to the world as *The Hobbit*, and which later led to the creation of his master work, *The Lord of the Rings*.

It is worth noting that Tolkien had no desire to be a 'children's author', as we usually define it, once stating that he had no particular interest in writing for children.[80] Yet, as we have seen, he did have an interest in four children, in particular, John, Michael, Christopher, and Priscilla Tolkien. To them, not to children considered as a target readership, he gave his ever-expanding gift for tale-spinning. His views on writing for children,

---

[80] See *The Letters of J. R. R. Tolkien*, ed. Humphrey Carpenter (Boston: Houghton Mifflin Company, 1981), p. 297.

however, did change over the years. When he wrote The Hobbit, for example, he was still under what he saw as a modern fallacy – the idea that fairy tales are especially, or perhaps uniquely, for children. In his famous essay, 'On Fairy-Stories,' Tolkien attacked that notion, and his more mature reflection resulted in the fairy-story known as The Lord of the Rings.

Tolkien's approach turns modern wisdom on its head. His children's writings would probably be judged, to some extent, as 'over the heads' of most children (sadly, there may be some hint of truth in this) because of the vocabulary and perhaps even the themes. On the other hand, The Lord of the Rings, certainly much more of an adult book than its predecessor, and, by the author's own admission, not written for children in particular at all, seems, nevertheless, to hold an appeal for children. Tolkien once wrote that he had heard of even young children reading or listening to The Lord of the Rings, and expressed his hope that it would help build their vocabularies.[81] As a life-long reader of Tolkien, I can testify to both the appeal to children, and the aid to vocabulary. I had read The Hobbit (far and away the favourite book of my youth) some nine times by the time I was twelve, at which tender age I read The Lord of the Rings for the first time.

The worthiness of the children's stories of Tolkien is in part a result of the covenantal context that led

---

[81] Ibid, 310.

to their creation – again, writing for the children of one's own blood rather than attempting to break into the market of kids' books. Writing stories for one's own children, however, is counter-intuitive in the Age of Specialists. Whereas modern child psychologists argue, in a sense, from universals to particulars ('this is what children, as a class, want and need; therefore, individual children, whoever they are, will like it'), Tolkien worked from particulars – his own children – to universals – children in general. That is, the stories were a success with John, Michael, Christopher, and Priscilla, who, as normal, typical children, turned out to be very good indicators of what millions of other children would like. Not, of course, that Tolkien told the stories as some kind of advance market research; he just wanted to delight his children. Because this was his aim, he was able to write stories that delighted many others as well.

FAMILY ACTIVITIES

1. Read the following short selections from well-known children's writings: Chapter Two ('In Which Pooh Goes Visiting and Gets Into a Tight Place') from *Winnie the Pooh* by A. A. Milne; Chapter Seven ('The Piper at the Gates of Dawn') from *The Wind in the Willows* by Kenneth Grahame; and *The Golden Key* by George MacDonald (this short story can be found in *The Gifts of the Child Christ*

and Other Stories and Fairy Tales, published by Eerdmans). Mom and Dad should read them first together; then read them to the children. Mom and Dad: ask yourself some questions. Do you believe your children will enjoy and understand these stories? What ages do you think they would need to be in order to get the most out of each one? Are there words, images, allusions, or concepts that are above children? Discuss these together and consider how you may be able to help your children see these elements as the stories are read as a family. (A hint or two to get you started: I once heard a university professor read from the Pooh story in a philosophy class, and certain sections from the chapter in *The Wind in The Willows* are often quoted in the context of theological discussion.) Do you see any moments in which the writers have 'written down' to children? How do these stories compare to more modern children's books with which you are familiar, and what differences or similarities do you see? Now, read these stories to your children. How do they respond to each one? What did they like? What did they not like? Which parts seemed difficult for them? Were you able to help them understand some of the elements that may have been above them? As with the fairy tales you read earlier, are there any similarities to the Christian story in these tales?

2. Get a copy of *How to Grow a Young Reader* by Kathryn Lindskoog and Ranelda Mack Hunsicker. Mom and Dad should read through

this together and take advantage of the excellent and extended recommended reading lists included in each chapter. Discuss ways in which you can encourage a love of reading and of good stories in your kids. Pay special attention to Chapter Two, 'The Enemies of Reading: High Tech Dragons.'

3. Along those lines, take stock of the amount of time you or your children spend with electronic amusements, especially video games and TV. Consider that the word 'amuse' literally means, 'no thought'. Make a conscious decision, not to improve the content of your television watching, but rather *to turn the thing off*. Use the time you have gained (what a wonderful gift!) to read the Scriptures, poetry, or stories to your children, or to simply talk to them, pray with them, and listen to them.

CHAPTER FIVE

TOLKIEN'S ROVERANDOM:
THE ORIGINAL TOY STORY

*You never know what will happen next, when once
you get mixed up with wizards and their friends.*[82]

J. R. R. tolkien, *Roverandom*

Roverandom, as mentioned earlier, was published twenty-five years after Tolkien's death, and was a story he made up to console his son, Michael, who had lost a favourite toy dog on the beach. Tolkien later wrote the story down, and drew several illustrations to go along with it. After the success of *The Hobbit*, Tolkien submitted the story, along with several others, to his publisher, Allen and Unwin. But precisely because of the success of *The Hobbit*, the story was not accepted for publication (though it received a good review

---

[82] J. R. R. Tolkien, *Roverandom* (Boston: Houghton Mifflin Company, 1998), 21.

from the publisher), as what Allen and Unwin really wanted from Professor Tolkien was more stories about hobbits. *Roverandom*, evidently, was never submitted for publication again, but after Tolkien's death, his popularity continued to rise, along with demand for his unpublished writings. So *Roverandom* finally saw print in 1998.

The story is simple enough. Rover, a dog who likes nothing better than playing with his ball in the garden of the lady who owns him, makes the mistake of speaking rudely to, and then biting the trousers of, an old man who, unfortunately for Rover, turns out to be a wizard named Artaxerxes.

The wizard's reaction is, perhaps, reasonable enough under the circumstances: 'Idiot! Go and be a toy!'[83] So poor Rover finds himself enchanted, turned into a toy dog sitting up in a begging position, which, you will admit, is a hard fate, even for a dog. Rover next finds that the wizard has put him in a toyshop, but a lady, who thinks he will be a wonderful toy for her little boy, soon buys him. In this, she is correct, though Rover has other ideas. He immediately sets his mind on running away (like all toys, he can move around at night), but finds himself unable to get out of the house. The next day, Rover, in the pocket of the little boy who is running along the beach with his brother, manages to get out of the pocket, and onto the beach.

---

[83] Ibid., 4.

From this point, Rover has a series of amazing adventures. He meets the sand-sorcerer, old Psamathos Psamathides (don't make him angry by forgetting to pronounce the *P* in each of his names), who sends him, on the back of a seagull, down the moon's path, and to the moon itself. There he meets the famous Man-in-the-Moon himself, and his dog, also named Rover (and who claims to be the oldest, and therefore the first dog ever named Rover, though he may in fact be exaggerating). The Man-in-the-Moon gives Rover wings, and renames him Roverandom (no doubt because of the many random adventures and travels of the little toy dog). Roverandom and the other Rover have many adventures, and are even chased by the Great White Dragon. Eventually, though, Rover returns to earth, seeking the wizard who turned him into a toy, so that he might apologise to him, and thereby, hopefully, be returned to his proper size. Artaxerxes however has married the daughter of the mer-king, and has gone to live under the sea, and to be the resident Magician in the Ocean. Roverandom journeys to the underwater kingdom in the belly of Uin, the oldest of the Right Whales. He meets Artaxerxes, but the magician is always too busy to change him back to his proper size. So Roverandom spends his time off on adventures with the palace dog (you guessed it: another Rover), including a run in with the ancient Sea-serpent.

You may be sure that there is a pleasant ending to the story of little Roverandom, but I don't want to tell everything that happens. This is a wonderful book to read aloud to your children, so find out for yourself. But for now, let's look at a few interesting things about the story that will help you and your children enjoy it more.

First, there are many references and allusions to fairy tales, myths, and nursery rhymes in the book. Humpty Dumpty, Old Mother Hubbard, King Arthur, and Spenser's The Faerie Queene are just a few. Some of the more prominent allusions include Jonah (Roverandom's ride in the whale), Pinocchio (the whale, as well as the fact that Roverandom is also a toy who wants to become 'real'), and Alice in Wonderland (some of the insects on the moon are reminiscent of those in Wonderland; also, at one point, Rover is given a bowl of water which bears the words, 'DRINK PUPPY DRINK,' which reminds us of the bottle Alice found, around the neck of which 'was a paper label, with the words 'DRINK ME' beautifully printed on it in large letters').[84]

It is interesting to note that Roverandom is unexpectedly (and yet we should have expected it, if we know anything about Tolkien at all) connected to Tolkien's other writings. If you are only familiar with the film versions of The Lord of the Rings, you may not know that these movies tell a story that is only a part of a larger mythology that Tolkien worked on nearly all his life (and never finished). The main narrative of this tale is told in

---

[84] Lewis Carroll, Alice in Wonderland (Ann Arbor, MI: Borders Classics, 2003), 8.

Tolkien's book *The Silmarillion*, and other parts of it are told in the twelve volume *History of Middle-earth* series, compiled and edited after Tolkien's death by his son, Christopher. *The Silmarillion* is the story of the creation of the world (if you read it, note the similarities to the biblical account of creation) and the history of the elves in Middle-earth. There are many references to *The Silmarillion* in *The Lord of the Rings* (even many that are kept in the movies, to the film-makers' credit), but surprisingly, even little Roverandom finds himself on the edges (literally) of that larger world. On one of his adventures travelling with the mer-dog and the old whale, Uin, Roverandom finds himself in 'Uncharted Waters' beyond all known lands. Soon, 'they passed the Shadowy Seas and reached the great Bay of Fairyland (as we call it) beyond the Magic Isles; and saw far off in the last West the Mountains of Elvenhome and the light of Faery upon the waves.'[85] In *The Silmarillion*, this is the Bay of Eldamar, the dwelling of the elves in Aman, the Blessed Realm, home of the angelic Valar. Note the similarity of the description in *Roverandom* to this passage from *The Silmarillion*: 'to the east it looked towards the Bay of Elvenhome, and the Lonely Isle, and the Shadowy Seas.'[86] As we discussed earlier, the scope of Tolkien's creative effort in his entire 'legendarium', as it is called, is simply breathtaking. In addition, it is a delightful

---

[85] *Roverandom*, 74.
[86] J. R. R. Tolkien, *The Silmarillion, Second Edition* (New York: Ballantine Books, 1977), 59.

surprise to find that even a simple story of a dog, told to comfort his son, is given the kind of creative attention that connects it to Tolkien's beautiful Christian mythology.

That however brings us to our next observation. Tolkien, a Christian writer, wrote what is certainly (and by his own admission) a Christian myth. Given the connection, however brief and fleeting, of *Roverandom* to that myth, is there any sense in which the adventures of Rover are also a Christian story? First, we must note that Tolkien was no writer of allegory. He wrote *Roverandom* to delight and cheer his son, not to weave a subtle, representative Christian story. Rover is not a symbol for any biblical character or truth. He is, within the sub-created world of the story, a real dog, who is really turned into a toy, and really has adventures at the edge of the world, on the Moon, and under the Sea.

Still, Tolkien was, after all, a Christian, and if his story rings true, it does so because it accurately reflects the created order, the world as God made it. All our creative efforts, as Tolkien himself clearly taught, are mere reflections of the true Creator, and our stories only have power to the extent that they creatively mirror His Story. Therefore, if we look hard enough, we can see Christian elements in *Roverandom*, which, though perhaps not put there purposefully by Tolkien for pedagogical ends, are still real enough. Remember Lewis's suggestion that a book may have more meanings than the author intends.

With that in mind, we can see several elements of Rover's story that mirror the Biblical account of God's dealings with man. First, it is fascinating to notice that Rover's adventures begin with a fall into sin, and that this fall even takes place in a garden, just as Adam fell into sin in the Garden of Eden (Genesis 3). Rover, playing with his ball in the garden, sins, both by word and deed, by his speech to the wizard, and by biting him as well. This sin, like Adam's, results in a changed nature. Rover is no longer a flesh-and-blood dog, but has become a metal toy, enslaved in a toyshop, and no longer enjoys the freedom and happiness of his original created state.

Second, Rover is 'redeemed' from this sin-cursed slavery when he is bought by the little boy's mother. 'You were bought at a price,' St Paul tells the church at Corinth, 'do not become slaves of men'.[87] Though he has been freed to live and be loved by the little boy, his new master, Rover does not realise this, and rejects it in the beginning. The story, in a sense, is the story of his 'conversion' to the New Life, a coming to love, for the first time, his new master.

Along the way, several wizards, especially the Man-in-the-Moon, aid Rover in his adventures. In Tolkien's mythology, wizards are angels. He took great care to distinguish them from what he called 'the vulgar devices of the laborious, scientific, magician'.[88] In Middle-earth, wizards are actually

---

[87] 1 Corinthians 7:23
[88] J. R. R. Tolkien, *Poems and Stories* (Boston: Houghton Mifflin Company, 1994), 122.

guardian angels.[89] Given the close relationship of even little *Roverandom* to Tolkien's mythology, we should think no different of the wizards we meet in this story. The Man-in-the-Moon, then, is an angelic servant of Iluvatar,[90] the One True God. As he is a divine servant, we see an added significance to the fact that the Man-in-the-Moon gives Rover the new name of Roverandom. The concept of a new name is a familiar biblical theme. 'The Gentiles shall see your righteousness, and all the kings your glory. You shall be called by a new name, which the mouth of the LORD will name.'[91] 'He who has an ear, let him hear what the Spirit says to the churches. To him who overcomes I will give some of the hidden manna to eat. And I will give him a white stone, and on the stone a new name written which no one knows except him who receives it'.[92]

Rover has a lot to learn before he will be able to accept the redemption that has been given to him. In the beginning he is a selfish, thoughtless dog, but through the story he begins to change. He learns courage, as he endures his many adventures and dangers. He learns the value of friendship with the moon-dog and the mer-dog, the Man-in-the-Moon and Uin, the whale. He learns courteous speech (rude language, you will

---

[89] See J. R. R. Tolkien, *The Letters of J. R. R. Tolkien*, ed. Humphrey Carpenter (Boston: Houghton Mifflin Company, 1981), 159.
[90] The Elvish name for God.

[91] Isaiah 62:2
[92] Revelation 2:17

remember, got him in this mess in the first place), love (for the little boy), loyalty, and even a wonder at the presence of beauty, as in the glimpse of Elvenhome in the last West. In the end, he must seek pardon for his sin in order to be restored. In the coming of that restoration, there is even a hint of Jesus's words, 'he who loses his life for My sake will find it',[93] as Rover, convinced he has lost that which he most loved, finds that there is more, a little more, to the story (I don't want to give away too much here, so you will need to read the book to understand what I mean).

Did Tolkien intend all of this just as I have described it? I honestly don't know, and to some extent, I doubt it. But Tolkien was not only a master writer, he was a Christian – a powerful combination – and his works reflect the reality of the world God made. The themes of sin, judgment, divine guidance, redemption, and sanctification are the patterns of life, and a good story – even a simple, light-hearted children's tale – will always reflect those patterns.

FAMILY ACTIVITIES

1. Read *Roverandom* as a family. Discuss the story together. Ask questions as you go. How did Rover's adventures begin? Was he to blame at all for his misfortunes?

---

[93] Matthew 10:39

2. As you go along, highlight some of the similarities of Roverandom to the Christian story as discussed in this chapter. Ask your children (certainly don't just outright tell them at first) if these elements seem familiar. Carefully lead them along in seeing the patterns and themes of the story. Point out the moral and theological elements of the story, and have the kids think of ways in which they have been (or could be) in similar situations.

3. Spend some time (perhaps in the car on a long trip, or on an afternoon during a family creative time) making stories of new adventures for Roverandom. A good place to start may be a story in which Roverandom meets with your own family dog (or cat!). Ask each child to contribute in some way to the story. Have them think of other interesting places Roverandom can visit (like the Moon and under the Sea in the book).

CHAPTER SIX

`FAMILY LORE`: TOLKIEN'S MR BLISS

It was now Mr Bliss's turn to laugh; and as he had not laughed since the day before yesterday, with nothing but bother in between, he laughed a lot.[94]

J. R. R. tolkien, *Mr Bliss*

If you have ever seen the popular TV show, *Home Improvement*, you know that one of the running gags of the show is that the main character, Tim 'the Tool Man' Taylor (played by Tim Allen), though obsessed with tools and cars, is actually rather graceless with them. He is forever causing some kind of serious mishap: catching something on fire with his propane torch, hitting someone on the head with a hammer, or managing to destroy his car. In one episode, while operating a crane at a construction site, Tim drops a huge metal beam onto his wife's car, completely wrecking it.

---

[94] J. R. R. Tolkien, *Mr. Bliss* (Boston: Houghton Mifflin Company, 1983), 42.

Though I cringe to admit it, I had my own 'Tool Man' moment some years ago. At that time, my wife and I lived in a community where all the mailboxes were centrally located, right beside a lake. I probably should mention that I had had a wreck in the car (not my fault, though!) not long before, and the front end was completely smashed in. I had bought a new car, but, being unable to actually get the car for a few days (I forget why, now), I had to drive the wrecked car for a short while before picking up the new one. On the last day before I was to get the new vehicle (and thus the last day I would ever have to drive the old, smashed-up car), I was stopped by a policeman and ticketed for driving without a front headlight. Sullen and discouraged over this turn of events, I continued home, stopping to get the mail on the way.

I pulled up to the mailboxes, opened the door and got out, leaving the door open, since this would only take a few moments. I retrieved my mail, and turned around.

The car was nowhere to be seen.

I ran out into the parking lot in time to see my car, rushing downhill, the door swinging open wildly. The steering wheel was evidently doing its bit as well, for the car jerked suddenly to the right, dropped down a steeper hill (the swinging door striking a tree on the way down) and finally plunged into the lake.

I'm not making this up.

I am not sure what happened. Obviously, I did not have the emergency brake on, but I did think

I had the gears disengaged. Either I am wrong about that, or it slipped into gear, somehow, but whatever the cause, in the lake she went. After wading through the shallow waters of the lake, and retrieving my soggy belongings from the car, I walked home, made a phone call, and duly paid a towing service to pull the poor vehicle from its watery resting place. I did manage to sell the car, eventually, to someone who needed some of the parts. Believe it or not, the thing actually drove a time or two more before taking its final journey and resting at the end of all its labours. Though no one was hurt by the accident, needless to say, it was not one of my better days.

It was a series of auto-mishaps that led J. R. R. Tolkien to write *Mr Bliss*, a story about the adventures of a man who wakes up one day and decides to buy a motor-car. Tolkien's official biographer, Humphrey Carpenter, described Tolkien's own driving as 'daring rather than skilful'.[95] According to Carpenter, Tolkien's driving philosophy and techniques eventually led his wife, Edith, to refuse to ride with him altogether. 'When accelerating headlong across a busy main road in Oxford in order to get into a side-street, he would ignore all other vehicles and cry, *'Charge 'em and they scatter!'* – and scatter they did.'[96]

Mr Bliss is an interesting character, described by Tolkien as living in a house with a high front

---

[95] Humphrey Carpenter, *J. R. R. Tolkien: A Biography* (Boston: Houghton Mifflin Company, 2000), 162.
[96] Ibid.

door, and tall rooms (naturally, because Mr Bliss likes to wear tall hats). In fact, he looks rather like a clown, a fact that we will have something to say about presently. Having donned his green top-hat one fine morning, Mr Bliss immediately says, 'I will go and buy a motor-car!'[97] And so he does, purchasing a bright yellow (inside and out) automobile from Mr Binks. The car is priced at five shillings, but when Mr Bliss asks for red wheels, he is informed that this feature will cost him an extra sixpence. Mr Bliss has left his purse at home, so Mr Binks kindly allows him to take the car, on condition that he leaves his bicycle (no pedals, as Mr Bliss only ever rides downhill) behind. Mr Bliss agrees, gets into the car, and the adventures begin.

He decides to visit the Dorkinses, evidently to show off (for they are 'disgustingly rich'[98]). On the way, he manages to hit two people (in two separate accidents) with his new car: Mr Day and Mrs Knight. Since he has injured them, Mr Bliss loads them into his car, along with their cabbages, bananas, and Mrs Knight's donkey (tied to the back). They proceed down the road and are hi-jacked by the bears who live in the forest: Archie, Teddy, and Bruno. As Mr Bliss's unlucky stars would have it, they happen to like cabbages and bananas (and motor-car rides) very much indeed. The adventures continue, but I won't spoil the whole story for you. They do meet the Dorkinses,

---

[97] *Mr. Bliss*, 7.
[98] Ibid., 36.

and a carload of trouble, involving the bears, the Dorkinses, a fantastic creature called a girabbit (more on this later), and, especially, Mr Bliss's ill-fated motor-car.

There are a number of interesting features to this story, most of them humorous in nature. First, there is Mr Bliss. Tolkien himself drew and coloured the illustrations for the book, and his drawings of the story's hero make him look rather like a clown. Is there any significance to this? According to Carpenter, Tolkien eventually sold his car and stopped driving altogether. Fuel rationing at the beginning of World War II made it difficult to justify keeping the car, but there was another reason. Carpenter writes: 'Tolkien perceived the damage that the internal combustion engine and new roads were doing to the landscape, and after the war he did not buy another car or drive again.'[99] One wonders whether Tolkien's increasing disapproval of motor-cars inspired (if that is the right word) his portrayal of Mr Bliss. Perhaps the visual rendering of him as clownish expresses Tolkien's dim view of those who drive cars (and of himself when he had engaged in an activity he would later come to see as foolish and destructive). It is certainly true that nothing but trouble comes of the decision to buy the vehicle, though whether Mr Bliss ever comes around to Tolkien's teetotaler approach to cars, I will not say. For that, you shall have to read for yourself.

---

[99] *J. R. R. Tolkien: A Biography*, 162.

The *girabbit* I mentioned earlier is also worthy of a few words. As you might guess, this fantastic creature is a combination of *giraffe* and *rabbit*, and Tolkien draws him essentially with the body and neck of a giraffe and the head of a rabbit. The girabbit plays an important part in the story, as you will see. But it is also an example of Tolkien's otherworldly imagination, at work even in a simple children's story inspired by light-hearted family memories. Given what we know of Tolkien, it is no surprise to find even the humdrum, commonplace world of Mr Bliss somehow on the edges of *Faerie* itself.

When we looked at *Roverandom*, we noted that Tolkien's larger mythology of the elves and Middle-earth found its way into the story. Do we find the same thing here? Well, yes, sort of, but not quite in the same way. There is a scene in the town in which lots of people have gathered to see what all the excitement is about (read the book!). As Carpenter notes, Tolkien, in a certain sense, wrote the story around the pictures he drew. In several places in the book, he describes what is going on in the pictures, and this is one of the times he does so. Among the many gathered, doing this and that, he takes note that '*old Gaffer Gamgee* is trying hard to hear'.[100] Many readers of *The Lord of the Rings* will know the name 'Gaffer Gamgee'. The Gaffer is the father of Samwise Gamgee, Frodo's faithful servant and

---

[100] *Mr. Bliss*, 37, emphasis added.

friend. Actually, Tolkien had made up the name while the family was on holiday at Lamorna Cove in Cornwall. A 'curious' old man, who would go around talking gossip and weather, was named 'Gaffer Gamgee' by Tolkien to entertain his children. As he put it, the name found a place in the Tolkien 'family lore' and was attached to anyone who resembled the original Gaffer.[101]

'Family lore': so much of Tolkien's inventive imagination was inspired by the covenantal context of his home and family. This is the central lesson, if any, of Mr Bliss. There are no epic battles between good and evil, and no thunderous moral points to be made (unless it be a kind of oblique warning about the dangers of motor-cars). Of course, there are fundamental moral assumptions that Tolkien works with, even in this tale (consciously, as a Christian writer, though non-Christian writers must often un-consciously borrow such assumptions). The moral concepts of right and wrong are assumed throughout, as many of the characters are wronged, in one way or another, and demand restitution (often at the expense of poor Mr Bliss, whose financial entanglements as a result of this adventure render him unable to take a summer holiday). We can also learn from Tolkien the value of a somewhat sceptical attitude toward new technology. There is nothing wrong with owning a car, but too often we become

---

[101] See J. R. R. Tolkien, *The Letters of J. R. R. Tolkien*, ed. Humphrey Carpenter (Boston: Houghton Mifflin Company, 2000), 347-348.

clowns like Mr Bliss, feverishly desiring the latest invention or convenience, without stopping to ask what effect this new gadget will have on our lives and families. But the main 'point' of the story is simply to entertain through humorous adventures, and the memory of the 'family lore' that inspired them. The humour is simple, almost childlike. At the end of the story (this is the only aspect of the ending I will reveal), Mr Day and Mrs Knight get married, and open up a green-grocer's shop and call it 'Day and Knight's.'[102] The family lore is central – both the little elements, like the name Gaffer Gamgee,[103] and the larger inspiration of Tolkien's own crashes and close shaves in a motor-car.

This is what the story-telling culture of a family should look like. Not all of us will write down our memories and stories in a book – though it may be good to put them on paper anyway, to have

---

[102] *Mr. Bliss*, 45. I have also wondered (Note: don't read this if you haven't read the book) whether there is perhaps a shrewd little allegory in *Mr. Bliss* involving these two characters (Tolkien, though no fan of allegory, wrote at least one: *Leaf, by Niggle*). Just as Mr. Bliss injures Mr. Day and Mrs. Knight with his car, so Tolkien viewed the advent of the "horseless carriage" as something that disrupted both Day and Night in otherwise peaceful shires everywhere. And, as at the end of the story, after Mr. Bliss has got rid of the car, Mr. Day and Mrs. Knight are married, so the elimination of motor-cars, in Tolkien's view, would restore peace and harmony to both Day and Night. Also, Mr. "Bliss," who is anything but blissful during the story, returns to a state of bliss by the end, again, after the departure of the motor-car. But I'm not certain about this. The story is enjoyable either way, though.

[103] Other hobbit-names appear in *Mr. Bliss*: Boffin, Fattie, Sam, etc.

something to hand down to future generations – but we will all tell stories from our 'family lore' around the supper table in the evenings, in the living room at Christmas, or while walking on the beach on holiday. We should encourage and develop this kind of tradition, and learn how to incorporate good books like *Mr Bliss* into our family lore. That is the most important thing we can learn from Mr Bliss. That is enough.

And that is all.

FAMILY ACTIVITIES

1. Around the dinner table, talk about your 'family lore'. What are some of the memories, fun or otherwise, that have shaped your family's identity? Are there certain words, phrases, or names that have taken on special significance, like 'Gaffer Gamgee' for the Tolkien family? Re-tell some of the funny, touching, exciting, adventurous, or even sad stories of your family lore. What is it that makes each one so special? Are there any stories that, though they were bothersome or even sad or frightening at the time, you can now look back on with laughter or at least peace?

2. Have another family time in which everyone makes up additional adventures for Mr Bliss and his friends (perhaps one of the Dorkinses buys his car and new mishaps follow). Have the children think about each character and the way he or

she acts in the story. What strange adventures might happen to the bears, or Sergeant Boffin, or the girabbit, given what the story reveals about their personalities and character traits? Ask your children if they can think of anyone (maybe even themselves) who are at least a little like the characters in the book.

3. Think about some of the modern conveniences in your family's life, whether cars, TVs, mobile phones, microwaves, or anything else. Talk together with your children about the ways these devices have benefited you, but also ways in which they may have had a damaging impact on your family's life and time. Are there perhaps ways in which these things keep you apart? Think hard. Many of these things have been part of our lives so long we have to imaginatively consider life without them. (One wag suggested that central heating had destroyed the modern family, in that before its advent, families gathered around the fire in the central room, whereas now they may warmly depart to their individual rooms – usually with their own TVs, phones, and the like.) In many cases, getting rid of such things may not be practicable, but at least discuss ways to keep them in their proper place: as servants, not masters.

CHAPTER SEVEN

ELVEN EPISTLES: TOLKIEN'S THE
FATHER CHRISTMAS LETTERS

*Goodbye now. I shall soon be off on my travels once
more. You need not believe any pictures you see of
me in aeroplanes or motors. I cannot drive one, and
I don't want to; and they are too slow anyway (not
to mention smell), they cannot compare with my own
reindeer, which I train myself. They are all very well
this year, and I expect my posts will be in very good
time. I have got some new young ones this Christmas
from Lapland.*[104]

J. R. R. tolkien,
The Father Christmas Letters

Snow is falling and the clouds are thick
overhead. The wind is mild but constant. It
is Christmas Eve morning, 1933. In a little house

---

[104] J. R. R. Tolkien, *The Father Christmas Letters* (Boston: Houghton
Mifflin Company, 1976), letter for 1931.

at 20 Northmoor Road, Oxford, four children are going about their daily activities, their hearts aglow with the light of the Christmas season, now upon them in earnest. The two eldest children, both boys, are off reading. The younger two – a nine-year old boy, and his four-year old sister – are playing quietly in the front room.

A noise at the front door causes them to look up. They are quiet for a few moments, listening intently, but no other noise is heard. Then they begin to smile, and both jump up together and run to the door. They open it cautiously and look outside. There is no one to be seen, but on the front mat, dusted with fresh snow, there lies a letter. The boy takes it in his hands carefully, almost reverently, and carries it inside.

He and his sister soon find their elder brothers and show them the treasure. Then all four together go off to their father's study, to show him the letter. They regard the study as the most exciting room in the house. Books are everywhere, on every wall, from floor to ceiling, and in the centre of the study there is a great black stove, generating waves of comforting heat against the chill of the winter day. They find their father there, pen in hand, apparently absorbed in his writing, though in fact his face is red and he looks slightly winded. Christopher, the youngest boy, always interested in his father's work, glances at the papers on the desk, and reads the words, 'Then he began a long and secret labour, and he summoned all his lore, and his power, and his subtle skill; and at the end of all he made the Silmarils.'[105]

The man smiles at his children. 'Well, happy Christmas, my dears,' he says.

The children smile, but say nothing. Christopher steps forward and presents the letter to his father.

'What's this, eh?' The man receives the letter and looks intently at it. The envelope contains curious words here and there: 'haste' and 'deliver on Xmas Eve. F.C.' and 'By Elf Messenger.' There is even a drawing of the Messenger, running with letter in hand.

'It's a letter from Father Christmas!' exclaims Priscilla, the little girl, unable to contain her excitement.

Her father smiles at her. 'Yes, it certainly appears to be. Got here just in time, too. But to tell you the truth, I'm dreadfully busy just now, so perhaps we'll just save this for later....' He begins to lay the letter on a stack of mail on the desk.

Shouting and giggling at once, the two younger ones leap onto their father's lap, trying to retrieve the letter and convince him to set about at once recovering his wits. The older brothers also join in on the fun, and soon all are laughing and playing, the festive spirit of the season washing over them in pure joy. The children's mother appears at the door, a great smile on her face, knowing what is taking place, and enjoying each moment. At last, the father, convinced of the urgency of the

---

[105] J. R. R. Tolkien, *The Silmarillion, Second Edition* (New York: Ballantine Books, 1977), 69.

matter, straightens his waistcoat, dons his glasses, and opens the letter. His daughter sits on his lap while the others stand around him, reading over his shoulder. He glances over the letter a moment before reading it aloud.

'My word!' he says. 'It seems Father Christmas has had his hands full this year. Just listen to this:

> My dears
> Another Christmas! And I almost thought at one time (in November) that there would not be one this year. There would be the 25th of December, of course, but nothing from your old great-great-great-etc. grandfather at the North Pole. My pictures tell you part of the story. *Goblins*. The worst attack we have had for *centuries*.[106]

As a child, did you ever write a letter to Father Christmas (or Santa Claus as we call him in America)? Perhaps your children have. Imagine getting a reply! Such was the fortunate circumstance of the four Tolkien children, who received a letter from Father Christmas each year for over twenty years, until the youngest had begun to 'grow up'. A time came when Father Christmas sent his final letter, though he promised they'd hear from him again, some day: 'Now I shall have to say "goodbye",

---

[106] *The Father Christmas Letters*, letter for 1933

more or less: I mean, I shall not forget you. We always keep the names of our old friends, and their letters; and later on we hope to come back when they are grown up and have houses of their own, and children….'[107] Legend has it that the letters were really written by J.R.R. Tolkien, the children's father, but they certainly seem convincing enough. One thing is certain: Father Christmas wrote of goblins and elves (including one named Ilbereth, which sounds a lot like "Elbereth", one of the angelic Valar in Tolkien's story, *The Silmarillion*), and so did Tolkien. But whether Father Christmas got these ideas from Tolkien, or Tolkien got them from Father Christmas, we may never know.

Tolkien's life was very much centred on his family. Though always busy with his academic work, or his writings, he delighted in spending time with his four children. Tolkien's daughter, Priscilla, would later remember that her father's study was always open to the children, except when he was teaching, of course. In his book *J. R. R. Tolkien's Sanctifying Myth*, Tolkien scholar Bradley J. Birzer writes: 'When Tolkien needed to work to make deadlines, he usually did so late at night, after his children were asleep.'[108] This was partly a personal preference: C. S. Lewis once remarked that Tolkien had a sort of 'horror of going to bed', though this meant that he 'was always best after midnight'.[109]

---

[107] *The Father Christmas Letters*, 'The Last Letter'.
[108] Bradley J. Birzer, *J. R. R. Tolkien's Sanctifying Myth: Understanding Middle-earth* (Wilmington, DE: ISI Books, 2003), 5.
[109] Ibid, 6.

But no doubt it was also a good way to get the work done without taking unnecessary time away from his family. Lewis once described him as 'the most married man he knew'.[110]

For many families with children, Christmas is the most exciting time of year, and presents and Santa are a big part of that. The Tolkiens were no different in that respect. Many Christians, however, are uneasy with the Santa/Father Christmas mythology, and fear, first, that it will displace the true story of Christ's birth (a justified fear), and second, that they will damage their children by 'lying' to them about Santa Claus.

There is no doubt that for many in our culture, Santa, reindeer, Rudolph, Frosty the Snowman, and the 'Winter Holiday' have overshadowed or completely replaced any understanding of Christmas as a memorial of Christ's Advent. This however is not in itself reason to discard these elements. Anything may be abused and become an idol; indeed, it is usually good things that are made into idols, whether wood, stone, pleasure, food, or recreation. Each church and family is responsible for properly emphasising the truth of Christmas and keeping other elements in their proper place.

As to the concern over 'lying', I am struck by how similar this criticism is to that expressed regarding myths and fairy tales in general. C. S. Lewis himself, in his younger days, before he had come to embrace Tolkien's view of mythology, once told his friend that myths were no more than 'lies

---

[110] Ibid, 8.

breathed through silver'.[111] But we have already seen that myths express a great deal of truth. The fact that an elf named Elrond or a centaur named Glenstorm never actually lived does not diminish the truth, goodness, and beauty expressed in the stories in which those creatures are found.

Though it is true that the modern Santa is grossly commercialised and far removed from the simple tales once told of him, there are yet elements of truth in the Father Christmas mythology. First, there is the archetype for the stories – St Nicholas, bishop of Myra. His true-life generosity gave rise to the legends of Santa Claus (a linguistic corruption of 'Saint Nicholas'). Moreover, the heart of the story is the giving of gifts, which mirrors the gift of God's grace in the birth, life, death, resurrection, and ascension of His Son. If these elements can be emphasised, and the greedy toy-lust overcome (and it *can* be done), then the story of Santa may be a good part of a family's mythological lore. Of course, this means that certain of the worse aspects of the modern Santa, particularly those that ascribe to him the attributes of Deity ('He sees you when you're sleeping, he knows when you're awake') should be cheerfully cast away. I have also found it helpful, even necessary, to leave out the whole 'naughty and nice' thing, whereby 'good' children get presents and bad ones get coal in their stocking. Let's be honest: parents who tell their children they

---

[111] J. R. R. Tolkien, "On Fairy-Stories," in *Tree and Leaf: Including the Poem Mythopoeia, The Homecoming of Beorhtnoth* (London: Harper Collins Publishers, 2001), 54.

won't get presents if they do something bad *are* lying to their children. Besides, if we make it clear that Christmas presents are gifts of grace, we more closely mirror the story of Christ, in which sinful humans got the last thing they deserved: a Saviour.

It is in this context, I believe, that *The Father Christmas Letters* can be received and enjoyed. Father Christmas can be presented as a mythological servant of Christ, as C. S. Lewis does in *The Lion, the Witch and the Wardrobe*. In that book, the White Witch has all Narnia under a spell so that it is always winter, but never Christmas. When Aslan returns to Narnia, the spell begins to break, and the first sign of this is the arrival of Father Christmas, gifts in hand. As he leaves, he shouts out, 'Merry Christmas! Long live the true King!'[112] In his *Letters to Children*, a child has written to Lewis, asking him to tell Aslan's other name. (In *The Voyage of the 'Dawn Treader'*, Aslan tells the children that he has another name in our world, and that they must learn to know him by that name.) Lewis wrote back, giving the child several hints as to Aslan's other name. Among other things, he asks if the child knows of anyone from our world who 'arrived at the same time as Father Christmas'.[113] So, for Lewis, the inclusion of Father Christmas in the story (several of his friends did not like this, and urged him to remove Father Christmas from the book, but Lewis refused) is to point to the

---

[112] C. S. Lewis, *The Lion, the Witch and the Wardrobe*, (New York: Harper Collins Publishers, 1950), 105.

[113] C. S. Lewis, *Letters to Children*, ed. Lyle W. Dorsett and Marjorie Lamp Mead (New York: Simon and Schuster, 1985), 32.

identity of Aslan. The late Kathryn Lindskoog, who began studying and writing about C. S. Lewis in the 1950s, has suggested that, in *The Chronicles of Narnia*, just as The Emperor over the Sea (Aslan's father) represents God the Father, and Aslan himself represents God the Son, so Father Christmas, the giver of gifts, also represents Someone. 'Those who know the New Testament well enough know which member of the Trinity is the giver of spiritual gifts in our own world. It is the Holy Spirit.'[114]

Tolkien's *Father Christmas Letters* are wholly light-hearted, and the book rather reminds me of *Roverandom*, both because of Tolkien's wonderful drawings that accompany the books, and because of the fun, fantastic things that happen in each. The Man in the Moon, for example, appears in both books, and his presence, as well as other elements, give *The Father Christmas Letters* the feel of a nursery rhyme come to life. The North Polar Bear, though he means well, is constantly causing trouble for poor Father Christmas: turning on the 'Rory Bory Aylis' fireworks (the Northern Lights), which turns the North Pole black, shakes the stars out of place, and breaks the moon into four; breaking the North Pole and crashing through Father Christmas's roof; and falling asleep in the bath with the water running, causing the water to leak through to the floor below, getting many of the presents wet. Sometimes, Father Christmas was so upset by the happenings that Ilbereth the Elf had to write the letters.

---

[114] Kathryn Lindskoog, *Journey Into Narnia* (Pasadena, California: Hope Publishing House, 1998), 112.

The Father Christmas Letters also contains glimpses (as we might expect) of Tolkien's invented mythology. For one thing, Ilbereth the Elf writes a few lines in Elvish, one of Tolkien's invented languages. Tolkien's love of languages, and of inventing new ones, could not help but find a way into these letters: the North Polar Bear (whose name is revealed as Karhu) invents an alphabet based on markings he had seen while lost in the Goblin caves. Also, we are told that the reason for the North Polar Bear's sometimes bad English spelling is the fact that he speaks *Arctic*, the language of the North Pole. The book even includes a sample of this language. One of the fun features of the book is that both the Goblin alphabet and the letter Karhu wrote with it are included. Children can use the alphabet to translate the letter.

Would that all children's literature was like these *Letters!* Writing for one's own children, as we have discussed, gives such books a covenantal context that makes them all the more valuable, for they don't just entertain us: they remind us of our own real, flesh and blood children, with names like Grace and William. They remind us of our need to tell our children stories, and to delight them as we teach them. They remind us to light a fire in our children's imaginations, with colour and light, laughter and silliness, splendour and nobility. Christmas is a season that naturally lends itself to such awakenings, and it is well worth our time to consider this year how we might best go about such worthy labour.

FAMILY ACTIVITIES

1. Begin to make Christmas as Christ-centred as possible. If you have never done this before, take the time to observe Advent next Christmas: this is the season in the Church Year of preparation for the birth of Christ. Simple Advent books are available to give you a plethora of ideas (a good one to begin with is *Christ in Christmas: A Family Advent Celebration*, published by Navpress, and including contributions from James Dobson, Chuck Swindoll, James Boice, and R. C. Sproul). Many of these books have family devotions for each Sunday of Advent, along with Christmas Carols and Scripture readings. An Advent wreath with candles is a well-known tradition for celebrating the Season. New candles are lit each week, each symbolising a different part of the story. That is the key thing to remember: Advent, like all the holy days and feast days in the Christian year, is about *telling a story*. This story, of course, is the greatest of all those we tell our children as we create a storytelling culture in our family. Each family is a culture, with its own traditions, its own ways of doing the ancient things, so come up with other ways to keep this story in your hearts and minds during Advent and Christmas. My daughter enjoys hearing the Christmas story with the aid of a simple Nativity set. We put the Magi far off in the 'East' and the Shepherds on a nearby hill and imagine what that night must have been like.

2. Re-think what you tell your children about Santa Claus or Father Christmas. Reject the cultural idolatries that enthrone him as the King of Christmas. Come up with your own family version of the Santa Claus story, using the traditional tales as a starting point. Come up with ideas for who he is and why he gives gifts. Try to make your Santa myth consistent with Christian theology, but beware of confusing the stories: don't have Santa stop by on the First Christmas Night to give Baby Jesus a toy sword and a bike. Keep a clear line between fictional myths and the True Myth, so your children won't be confused, or worse, think the story of Christ is no truer than the fictional myths.

3. Try, as parents, or even as a family, writing a letter to the children from Santa or Father Christmas. Come up with humorous characters, like the North Polar Bear, and funny circumstances and trials for the denizens of the North Pole. Make it a tradition to write a new letter each year, with new adventures and mishaps. Take a page from Tolkien's playbook and incorporate famous Nursery Rhymes or Fairy Tale characters into the story. Read *The Father Christmas Letters* aloud and enjoy the bright pictures and creative stories. Pick up a copy of *The Father Christmas Letters* on CD or audiotapes (the unabridged version read by Derek Jacobi is wonderful). Incorporate fun stories like these into your Christmas celebrations, but make it a decidedly *minor* part – do not forget where the focus should be.

CHAPTER EIGHT

LUCK AND PROVIDENCE IN TOLKIEN'S THE HOBBIT

'A very good tale!' said he. The best I have heard for a long while…You may be making it all up, of course, but you deserve a supper for the story all the same.'[115]

J. R. R. tolkien, *The Hobbit*

What a delight it was to read *The Hobbit* again in preparation for this chapter! I believe I have mentioned before that this was by far my favourite book as a child, one I read many times. I remember watching the Rankin/Bass animated production of *The Hobbit*, which came out when I was about seven or eight. We had the LP record of the production, which included the entire music and dialogue track from the film, so that listening to the record was like watching

---

[115] J. R. R. Tolkien, *The Hobbit* (Boston: Houghton Mifflin Company, 1966), 135.

the movie with your eyes closed. I listened to it so many times I still have nearly all of it memorised. It was the definitive story of my youth, and this is no small miracle: in the culture of the 1970s and 1980s, a culture awash in super-heroes, teen idols, rock bands, and TV stars, my heroes were dwarves, eagles, elves, a wandering wizard, and a hobbit. *The Hobbit* is the masterpiece of Tolkien's children's books and, like the others, was first told to his own children, before it was written down.

Just what is a hobbit? Perhaps no answer is required in our day, for hobbits have been everywhere for the last five years or more, with the world-wide excitement leading up to, and during the theatrical domination of, the film versions of *The Lord of the Rings*, which as many know is the sequel to *The Hobbit*. Hobbits are what some call 'little people', but don't confuse them with dwarves or (especially!) 'fairies'. They are nothing at all like what Tolkien called 'that long line of flower-fairies and fluttering sprites with antennae that I so disliked as a child, and which my children in their turn detested.'[116] Hobbits are small (though not as small as the modern fairies), a little smaller than even dwarves, but very different. They are entirely domesticated, rustic, and, as Tom Shippey has argued in *J. R. R. Tolkien: Author of the Century*, very, very English. Very *modern* English, even: Shippey notes a number

[116] J. R. R. Tolkien, "On Fairy-Stories," in *Tree and Leaf: Including the Poem Mythopoeia, The Homecoming of Beorhtnoth* (London: Harper Collins Publishers, 2001), 6.

of anachronisms that place Bilbo and other hobbits squarely in the world of upper middle-class, twentieth-century England. Bilbo is used to having his meat delivered fresh from the butcher, he feels completely out of sorts without a pocket-handkerchief, and he looks down his nose at the very notion of adventures, especially as they tend to make one late for dinner.

It is this stay-at-home complacency that makes Bilbo both out of place in the high heroic world of the fairy-tale (into which he is so unceremoniously thrust by Gandalf) and an apt voice for all of us moderns. Bilbo feels how we would feel in such a world. He misses his regular meals and his quiet home and fireplace, and often wonders what he is doing on one of those horrible adventures he has heard so much about.

What adventure? There have been rumours of an eventual movie version of *The Hobbit*, perhaps directed by Peter Jackson (Oscar-winning director of *The Lord of the Rings* films), but in case you can't wait that long, here is a rough sketch of the story. Gandalf the wizard shows up at Bilbo's hobbit-hole in Hobbiton one Tuesday morning, inviting him on an adventure. Bilbo tries to get rid of him, but (flustered as he was) invites him to tea the next day. On Wednesday, Gandalf shows up for tea with thirteen dwarves, led by the great Thorin Oakenshield, grandson of Thror, King Under the Mountain. The dwarves and Gandalf ask Bilbo to join them in their quest to reclaim the treasure stolen from them many years before by Smaug, the great dragon. Thorin's people had lived in Erebor, the Lonely Mountain, near the town of Dale, where men lived, and not far from the kingdom of the Wood-elves at the edge of Mirkwood forest. Smaug had killed many men and dwarves, and destroyed Dale, and had lain on the mound of treasure (as dragons will do) ever since. Thorin was determined to take back the gold and the kingdom. Gandalf had suggested going secretly, by stealth, rather than marching with armies and banners against Smaug (a hopeless errand). He persuades him that Bilbo must come, that the quest cannot succeed without him.[117] And Bilbo does come, though he hardly knows why at the time.

Each new chapter for the first half of the book introduces some new inhabitants of the world of the fairy-tale, as Shippey has pointed out: dwarves and a wizard (chapter one), trolls (chapter two), elves (chapter three), goblins (chapter four), Gollum (chapter five, though Gollum is an original creation of Tolkien's); wargs (or evil wolves; chapter six); Beorn (a man who sometimes takes the shape of a bear; chapter seven); giant spiders (chapter eight). Bilbo is drawn progressively into this world through his many adventures, and the style becomes more and more heroic and archaic as the book moves on. We pass from the warm domesticity of Bilbo's hobbit-life, to wayside

---

[117] See J. R. R. Tolkien, *Unfinished Tales: The Lost Lore of Middle-earth* (New York: Ballantine Books, 1988), 335-340.

adventures with trolls and goblins, to, in the end, encounters with dragons, and epic battles (the Battle of Five Armies). Along the way, Bilbo proves again and again that, as Gandalf had said, there was much more about him than even he knew. In the darkness near Gollum's underground lake, Bilbo finds a magic ring that makes him invisible. Earlier, in the trolls' cave, he had claimed an ancient elvish sword. These tools, along with his own wits and resourcefulness, win the respect of the dwarves such that, by the end of the adventure, Bilbo has in fact become the leader of the party. (Gandalf had left before they entered Mirkwood Forest, but even Thorin increasingly looked to Bilbo for guidance.) Bilbo saves them from the spiders, and rescues them from the Wood-elves' prison. He is notable for (as Thorin puts it) 'courage and resource far exceeding his size,' not to mention 'good luck far exceeding the usual allowance'.[118]

This quality of *luck* deserves special thought and attention, for it comes up again and again in the story. After he saved them from the giant spiders of Mirkwood, the dwarves observed, with some surprise, that Bilbo had, in fact 'some wits, as well as luck and a magic ring – and all three are very useful possessions.'[119] Bilbo, giving himself various riddling names while speaking to Smaug, calls himself both 'lucky number' and 'Luckwearer'.[120] 'I have begun to trust my luck

---

[118] *The Hobbit*, 224.
[119] Ibid, 177.
[120] Ibid, 235.

more than I used to in the old days,'[121] he says just before entering the tunnel that leads to Smaug's chamber, and later he tells the dwarves they 'have tempted luck too long!'[122] Luck is brought up often enough to make us pay attention. Shippey includes a discussion of luck in his chapter on *The Hobbit* in *Author of the Century*. 'This belief that luck is a *possession*, which one can own, and perhaps even give away or pass on, may seem to be characteristically dwarvish, i.e. old fashioned, pre-modern: it is a commonplace of Norse saga, for instance, where there are many lucky and unlucky cloaks, weapons, and people. But people do not think that way about luck any more. Or do they?'[123] They do, as Shippey points out, and as we know from experience. Modernity, the advances of science, the rapid-fire growth of technology – none of these have stamped out superstition. People still talk of 'luck' and (perhaps especially) 'chance' as if they are tangible substances or forces of nature: things that exist and can produce particular results in our lives.

Maybe the dwarves and little Bilbo are just more modern anachronisms, then. Shippey is right that luck fits in well with certain strands of the fairy-tale tradition, but it is strange, when you think of it, that it should also fit in well with our modern, 'enlightened' civilisation, which often spurns fairy-

---

[121] Ibid, 224.

[122] Ibid, 252.

[123] Tom Shippey, *J. R. R. Tolkien: Author of the Century* (Boston: Houghton Mifflin Company, 2000), 27.

tales as children's nonsense. But are we Christians any better? In some corners of the Church, 'prayer cloths' are thought to bring health and financial prosperity, while one must be careful not to speak 'negative words', which can bring about sickness, poverty, and all sorts of devastating ruin, including death. Is this so different from the notion of luck? I think not. Still, historic Christianity rejects any idea of an independent force or substance (be it luck, chance, or even 'faith') that controls or even influences the course of history, or the everyday lives of people, because such a force or substance would negate the possibility of a sovereign God ruling by miracle and providence in the world. But Tolkien was a Christian. What does this repeated invocation of luck in *The Hobbit* mean? Has Tolkien abandoned the Church's insistence on sovereignty and providence in favour of the lucky swords and cloaks of Norse myth?

We can begin to answer this question by looking closer at a couple of 'lucky' events in *The Hobbit*, both of which have to do with moments when Bilbo finds something. 'Finding' may be the result of purpose or intention, if one is looking for something specific, but in both these cases, Bilbo finds things that he was *not* looking for. We will take them in reverse order. Near the end of the story, Bilbo finds the Arkenstone of Thrain, the great jewel that is called 'the heart of the Mountain', and which Bilbo rightly says is also 'the heart of Thorin'.[124] Bilbo, perhaps under the

---

[124] *The Hobbit*, 284.

spell of the great treasure, hides it, telling no one. As the story makes plain, Bilbo is without doubt the least affected by the tremendous allure of the dragon-gold, but he is not wholly *un*affected. A little later, Thorin speaks to his companions, telling them that, of all the treasure, the Arkenstone is *his*, and he will be revenged on any who, finding it, withholds it. After the death of Smaug, the men of Lake-town, including Bard, the slayer of the Dragon, and the Elven-king, his friend, thinking Thorin and his companions dead, march with their armies to the Mountain, hoping to use the treasure to rebuild what Smaug has destroyed. They find, to their surprise, that Thorin and Company still live. They implore Thorin to bestow some of his treasure to help the people of the destroyed Lake-town, but Thorin refuses (the reasons for this are complex, and do not involve a simple refusal to help those in need, but we cannot go into those reasons now). War seems inevitable, for Thorin has sent messengers to his cousin Dain of the Iron Hills, to bring an army to help them. Bilbo, who has been promised by Thorin a fourteenth share of the treasure (once recovered) steals out one night, and delivers the Arkenstone to Bard and the Elven-king. They wonder, reasonably, how it is Bilbo's to give? Bilbo replies that he will forfeit his share of the treasure, and that Bard can offer to return the Arkenstone to Thorin for the delivery of Bilbo's share to Bard.

This is a noble act, a sacrificial act on Bilbo's part, to avoid war between those he believed ought to be friends, but Thorin, on finding out what happened, feels – understandably, I believe – betrayed. Still, Thorin was wise enough to see the intention and result of Bilbo's action, had he not let his anger control him at that moment. For in fact the only actual result of Bilbo's delivering the Arkenstone to Bard was that Bilbo himself would forfeit his share of the treasure: Thorin would give up nothing, for he would have received the Arkenstone back upon delivering Bilbo's fourteenth share (which he had already promised in any case). In other words, Bilbo had no intention of depriving Thorin of his heirloom, but only to avoid a pointless battle. We may also observe that it took great courage for Bilbo to tell Thorin (as he does) that it was he who had surrendered the Arkenstone, for he did not have to do so. (Bard and the others surely would not have told where they obtained it, realising the danger it could put Bilbo in.) Thorin's initial reaction, then, reasonable though it was, should have given way to understanding, in view of the nobility and courage of Bilbo's sacrifice. It did not, however, and Thorin's pride, and the Dragon-spell of the gold,[125] gets the better of him, causing him

---

[125] Tolkien explains: '[Bilbo] did not reckon with the power that gold has upon which a dragon has long brooded,' (*The Hobbit*, 276) and this, combined with the Dwarves' natural lust for gold, and of course the memory of the sorrows of his people caused by Smaug's theft of the gold, blinds Thorin to all else.

to utter harsh words he would soon regret. He flies into a rage, threatens to throw Bilbo off the high wall on which they are standing (whether he would have actually done so is debatable, but he is in fact prevented from doing this by the sudden reappearance of Gandalf), and orders Bilbo out of the Mountain at once, telling him in no uncertain terms that no friendship of his goes with the hobbit.

The question we must ask is, was the finding of the Arkenstone another example of Bilbo's unusual luck? Thorin, had he known, might have considered it so (before he knew what Bilbo would do with it), for, from his vantage point, the luckiest thing that could happen (apart from the death of Smaug) would be the finding of the Arkenstone. Bard and the Elven-king would perhaps agree, though for different reasons: the finding of the Arkenstone by Bilbo (as opposed to, say, Thorin), from their perspective, could not have been luckier, for it gave them the best bargaining lever imaginable to ensure they obtained the treasure they desired, and to avoid a war that neither wants.

From Bilbo's point of view, however, we would have to admit that the finding of the Arkenstone was not so lucky; indeed, we might be tempted to say this is the point in the story where his famous luck begins to fail. What does it get him? Insults and anger from his former friend, shame and pity from the dwarves, and in the end, a nasty knock on the head in a battle he had not been able to avoid anyway. For the fight between elves, dwarves, and men is cut short suddenly by the appearance of a vast army of goblins, and those who were ready to fight each other now become allies against the common enemy. Bilbo later realises the seeming pointlessness of the whole affair. '[Y]ou made a great mess of that business with the stone,' he says to himself, 'and there was a battle, in spite of all your efforts to buy peace and quiet.'[126] So: good luck or bad luck? We haven't really answered the question, but it is enough at this point if we can see that the question of whether something is indeed 'lucky' is not so obvious as it may at first appear.

We can shine a little more light on the subject, though, by taking a look at another 'lucky' turning point in *The Hobbit*. It is an obvious choice: Bilbo's finding of the Ring. I capitalise 'Ring' because, as many of you know, the ring Bilbo finds is *the* Ring: the One Ring, the Ruling Ring made by the Dark Lord Sauron (called the Necromancer in *The Hobbit*), and the cause of all the trouble in *The Lord of the Rings*. Of this Ring that Bilbo found, Tolkien penned this poem, the final lines of which are inscribed in invisible fiery letters on the Ring itself:

Three Rings for the Elven-kings under the sky,
Seven for the Dwarf-lords in their halls of stone,
Nine for Mortal Men doomed to die,

---

[126] *The Hobbit*, 301.

One for the Dark Lord on his dark throne
In the Land of Mordor where the Shadows lie.
One Ring to rule them all, One Ring to find them,
One Ring to bring them all and in the darkness bind
them
In the Land of Mordor where the Shadows lie.[127]

The finding of the One Ring (which has been missing for some two thousand years) by Bilbo is an event of the highest import, with far-reaching consequences, though Bilbo cannot see that at the time. The finding of the Ring affects no one more than Bilbo's nephew Frodo, to whom Bilbo gives the Ring many years later. For Frodo must take the Ring to Mordor to be destroyed. Frodo suffers greatly as the Ringbearer; indeed suffers wounds that this world can never fully heal. Why did he suffer so? Because, many years before, Bilbo's 'hand met what felt like a tiny ring of cold metal lying on the floor of the tunnel'.[128] A hobbit – who never wanted to be in such a place – is crawling under a mountain in the dark, and blindly puts his hand on a ring. And the world changes. It is difficult to imagine a more 'chance' encounter. 'Luck,' Bilbo thought it, and certainly the ring was very useful, saving both his life and the lives of the dwarves on more than one occasion. But was it only luck?

For Frodo, at least, the finding of the Ring is

---

[127] J. R. R. Tolkien, *The Lord of the Rings: The Fellowship of the Ring* (New York: Ballantine Books, 1965), vii.
[128] The Hobbit, 79.

anything *but* lucky. 'I wish it had never, never, been found' cries Frodo near the end of his journey.[129] Others in the story agree. 'I could wish, were it of any avail, that the One Ring had never been wrought, *or had remained forever lost*'[130] says Galadriel, the elf-lady of Lothlorien. Elrond Half-elven of Rivendell speaks similarly: 'For in the days of Isildur the Ruling Ring passed out of all knowledge, and the Three[131] were released from its dominion. But now in this latter day they are in peril once more, *for to our sorrow the One has been found.*'[132]

Clearly, what seemed so 'lucky' at first glance turned out to be anything but. This is the problem with Bilbo's pride in his unusual supply of luck: he is in fact a pragmatist. Pragmatism, a uniquely American contribution to philosophy, is structured around a simple idea: that which 'works' is always the right choice or the best thing that can happen. So for Bilbo, finding a magic ring 'works': it helps him out of many tight spots, so he considers it 'lucky'. One of the many problems with Pragmatism is that, as Gandalf put it, 'even the very wise cannot see all ends'.[133] That is, what seems to 'work' now – what seems to produce at the moment a desired goal – may in the long run be anything *but* productive. No one can foresee

[129] J. R. R. Tolkien, *The Lord of the Rings: The Return of the King* (New York: Ballantine Books, 1965), 199.

[130] *The Fellowship of the Ring*, 410, emphasis added.

[131] The Three Rings of the Elves.

[132] *The Fellowship of the Ring*, 275, emphasis added.

[133] Ibid, 65.

all the long-term consequences of their actions and choices. Luck suffers the same fatal wound as Pragmatism: it is defined by the moment, and the short-term benefits may be far outweighed by the long-term disasters.

But there is more to be said. We have thus far only talked about whether the finding of the Ring is 'good luck' or 'bad luck'. As we have seen, a case can be made that it was actually bad luck. Or was it? Gandalf, speaking of the evil nature of the Ring, suggests to Frodo that in fact, Gollum, who owned the Ring before Bilbo, did not merely lose the Ring – the Ring, filled with the malice and will of its dark maker, actually left Gollum. Frodo, perhaps finding this a bit much to believe, says, 'What, just in time to meet Bilbo?' Gandalf explains that the Ring was trying to get back to its Master, but that more than just this was going on. 'Behind that there was something else at work, beyond any design of the Ring-maker. I can put it no plainer than by saying that Bilbo was *meant* to find the Ring, and *not* by its maker. In which case you also were *meant* to have it. And that may be an encouraging thought.'[134]

The finding of the Ring by Bilbo, then, was *not* luck, either good or bad. It was *meant* to happen – and notice Tolkien's double emphasis on this word. There is intention, purpose, design, in the whole affair. Though Gandalf goes no

---

[134] Ibid, 61, italics in original.

further, it is worth remembering that, in Tolkien's legendarium, Gandalf is a *Maia*, an incarnate angel and servant of Eru, the One – God. It is God who *meant* Bilbo to find the Ring, and that means that, quite apart from the short-term benefits of Bilbo's use of the Ring, and despite the sorrows that the finding of the Ring brings to Frodo and the elves, the reappearance of the Ring was *meant*, ultimately, for good. This is obvious by the end of *The Lord of the Rings*, for the finding of the Ring has led to the downfall of Sauron, and victory in the War of the Ring. Bilbo, content at the thought of his 'lucky' find, could never have foreseen any of that.

If this is the case, then, why should Tolkien so emphasise Bilbo's abundance of luck in *The Hobbit*? Again, he was a Christian, and well aware of the difference between random luck and purposeful providence. There are indicators that there is more at work here in Tolkien's thinking. Colin Duriez and David Porter, in their helpful book *The Inklings Handbook*, opine that Bilbo 'seems to have extraordinary luck, but there is an underlying sense of providence at work in events.'[135] In Tolkien's posthumously published work, *Unfinished Tales: the Lost Lore of Middle-earth*, there is a short work entitled 'The Quest of Erebor,' which gives a good deal of background

---

[135] Colin Duriez and David Porter, *The Inklings Handbook: The Lives, Thought and Writings of C. S. Lewis, J. R. R. Tolkien, Charles Williams, Owen Barfield and Their Friends* (St Louis: Chalice Press, 2001), 125.

information for the story in *The Hobbit*. Here we learn of Gandalf's meeting with Thorin in Bree (a town outside the Shire where Bilbo lives) and of his effort to persuade Thorin to take Bilbo on the quest for Smaug's treasure. In the end, because Bilbo came on the quest, Smaug was defeated, the goblins were crushed, and the Kingdom Under the Mountain was restored. The scene in 'The Quest of Erebor' takes place after the downfall of Sauron in *The Lord of the Rings*, and it is a conversation between Gandalf, Frodo, and several others. Gandalf mentions the fact that, while they had been fighting Sauron in the south, Dain, King Under the Mountain, and King Brand of Dale (rebuilt after the Desolation of the Dragon), a descendent of Bard, had fought a great battle against Sauron's armies in the north. Gandalf considers how different things could have been:

> The main attack was diverted southwards, it is true; and yet even so with his farstretched right hand Sauron could have done terrible harm in the North...if King Brand and King Dain had not stood in his path. When you think of the great battle of Pelennor,[136] do not forget the battle of Dale. Think of what might have been. Dragon-fire and savage swords in Eriador! There might be no Queen in Gondor. We might now only hope

---

[136] The greatest battle of the War of the Ring, fought on the Pelennor fields outside the walls of Minas Tirith, the capital city of Gondor.

to return from the victory here to ruin and ash.
But that has been averted – because I met Thorin
Oakenshield one evening on the edge of spring
not far from Bree. A chance-meeting, as we say
in Middle-earth.[137]

'As we say in Middle-earth': Tolkien goes to the
trouble to qualify Gandalf's description of the
'chance-meeting'. But during the discussion
in 'The Quest of Erebor,' Gandalf has repeated
his words to Frodo that both he and Bilbo had
been *meant* to have the Ring, and adds that he,
Gandalf, was also *meant* to guide both Bilbo and
Frodo in all this. The point being made is that what
in Middle-earth is called a 'chance-meeting,' was
actually designed and determined for a specific
purpose, and eventually led to sorrow and joy,
both unforeseen.

Here again, 'chance,' like Bilbo's 'luck,' is really
nothing of the sort. 'I have now lived a hundred and
nine winters in this world and have never yet met
any such thing as luck.' So says Lewis's character
the Hermit of the Southern March in *The Horse and*

---

[137] J. R. R. Tolkien, *Unfinished Tales: The Lost Lore of Middle-earth* (New York: Ballantine Books, 1988), 340. Eriador was the vast area of land in what had once been the northern kingdom of Arnor (founded by the man of Numenor, Elendil, whose son Isildur would later cut the one Ring from the hand of Sauron). At the time of the War of the Ring, Eriador included the Shire (home of the hobbits), the town of Bree, and the Elven kingdom of Rivendell. Gandalf's words suggest that Arwen, daughter of Elrond, and now Queen of Gondor, might have been slain, and Rivendell and the Shire destroyed, and so they would have returned "to ruin and ash."

His Boy[138]. Does Tolkien agree? Gandalf himself reveals the truth, at the very end of *The Hobbit*. The book ends several years after Bilbo has returned home. Gandalf and Balin (one of the thirteen dwarves with whom Bilbo journeyed to the Lonely Mountain) come to visit him, and Balin tells Bilbo of all the wonderful changes that have happened in Dale and among the dwarves since the death of Smaug. Bilbo, thinking back to the prophecies he had heard while in Lake-town, of the restoration and rebuilding that would take place when the King Under the Mountain returned, remarks, with some surprise, that 'the prophecies of the old songs have turned out to be true, after a fashion!' 'Of course!' replies Gandalf. 'And why should not they prove true? Surely you don't disbelieve the prophecies, because you had a hand in bringing them about yourself? You don't really suppose, do you, that all your adventures and escapes *were managed by mere luck*, just for your sole benefit? You are a very fine person, Mr Baggins, and I am very fond of you; but you are only quite a little fellow in a wide world after all.'[139]

Tolkien, it seems, has been pulling our leg with all the talk of luck throughout the story. Notice Gandalf's words: Bilbo's adventures and escapes had not been, after all, 'managed by mere luck', and he should remember that he is only a little fellow in a wide world; that is, there are bigger

---

[138] C. S. Lewis, *The Horse and His Boy* (New York: Macmillan Publishing Company, 1954),143
[139] *The Hobbit*, 317, emphasis added.

things going on than just Bilbo's adventures, important though they are. There were providential reasons for Bilbo's escapes, for his finding of the Ring, and they had little (though not nothing) to do with Bilbo's own personal safety, and they had absolutely *nothing* to do with a fortunate overflow of something called 'luck'. Rather, they are events that were actually 'prophesied' – a loaded biblical and Christian term suggesting God's foreknowledge and purpose – many years in advance.

What a fine reminder for us! We too endure dangers and adventures (though not always of the same sort Bilbo faced) and we need to be reminded that these things are *meant* to happen, though not for our sole benefit. We are characters in a great story, and though at times it may seem to us we are the central character, we must remember that this is not the case. But though we are but minor characters in this story, the same providential hand that guides the epics of kings and warriors guides our little stories, with care and kindness, and with the attention that only a Master Storyteller can give.

FAMILY ACTIVITIES

1. Read *The Hobbit* together. Look for the references to luck, and talk about them as they arise. Find out what the children think of luck, if

indeed they have ever thought of it at all. As you explain to them how the idea of luck is used in our culture, or in past cultures, suggest to them that there may be more going on in *The Hobbit* than meets the eye. Ask them if they think 'good luck' can really cause things to go well or 'bad luck' can cause things to go wrong. Explore the Christian idea of providence, and how God guides us in our lives. Begin, as you read the story together, to point out the contradiction between a belief in luck and a trust in God's providence. Once you have finished the book, make sure to emphasise Gandalf's words about luck and prophecy at the end. Read the selection from *The Lord of the Rings*, quoted above, that suggests that Bilbo was meant to find the Ring, and talk to the children about Who it is that 'means' these things. Talk to them about the fact that what seems 'lucky' at first might not really be so lucky later on.

2. In creating the multi-faceted legendarium of Middle-earth (of which his friend Lewis said *The Hobbit* is merely the adaptation for children), Tolkien intended to create a mythology for England. He believed England had very little native mythology; most of the traditional stories being either imported or diluted by other cultures (mostly French). He hoped to *begin*[140] this mythology, with the idea that future generations would build upon it (as always happens with myths

---

[140] A crucial word: the heart of the mythology, *The Silmarillion*, was a book he worked on for sixty years, and never finished.

and legends), creating new stories, songs, poetry. Get the family together some evening and create your own additions to the Middle-earth story. If you and your children have read some of Tolkien's other Middle-earth stories (*The Silmarillion* or *The Lord of the Rings*) you will have more to go by, but *The Hobbit* is a fine place to start. Have everyone create a work of art related to Bilbo and his adventures. Let each do what he or she likes best: pencil sketch, finger-painting, poem, song, clay sculpture, or story. Someone can even cook a dish inspired by *The Hobbit*. (The first chapter has a lot of talk about food: cakes, eggs, raspberry jam, apple-tart, mince-pies, cheese, salad, coffee, cold chicken, pickles. In the house of Beorn there is lots of bread, butter, cream, and honey. The ability to cook is an artistic talent, involving not only flavour, but beauty as well). C. S. Lewis received many works of art based on *The Chronicles of Narnia*: usually pictures drawn of the characters by young readers, but in one case he received a statue of Reepicheep the Mouse (see *Letters to Children*). New stories can be created, either by individuals or by the whole family. Tolkien gives us some help: he notes that Bilbo and Gandalf had many adventures on the journey home, but these adventures are not chronicled in the book. Or think of things that might have happened to Bilbo in later years, or to some of the dwarves. Have everyone share their creations with the whole family, and allow everyone to give input, encouragement, and constructive criticism.

CHAPTER NINE

'WATCHFUL DRAGONS': THE CHILDREN'S WRITINGS OF C. S. LEWIS

Why did one find it so hard [as children] to feel as one was told one ought to feel about God or about the sufferings of Christ? I thought the chief reason was that one was told one ought to. An obligation to feel can freeze feelings. …But supposing that by casting all these things into an imaginary world, stripping them of their stained-glass and Sunday School associations, one could make them for the first time appear in their real potency? Could one not thus steal past those watchful dragons? I thought one could.[141]

C. S. LEWIS

*t*olkien, as we have seen, wrote children's stories within the covenantal context of his home and family. Lewis, for most of his life, had

---

[141] C. S. Lewis, *Of Other Worlds: Essays and Stories*, ed. Walter Hooper (San Diego: Harcourt Brace and Company, 1966), 37.

no children (he did gain two stepsons through his marriage late in life), and so could not write from the same perspective. He did admire the method of writing for particular children (one's own, usually), as he discusses in his essay, 'On Three Ways of Writing for Children.' As examples of those who wrote in this way, he mentions Lewis Carroll, Kenneth Grahame, and Tolkien. To this list we could add names like A. A. Milne, and George MacDonald. Lewis noted that in such storytelling, a new sense of community is formed, as the story (and the relational interaction) changes both parent and child.[142] Again, we see the covenantal foundation for the telling of tales within families.

But Lewis, again, could not write from that perspective, or not wholly. Lewis describes his own method as writing children's stories 'because a children's story is the best art-form for something you have to say'.[143] Still, though not a father himself, he had come to know various children and when he wrote children's stories, he wrote with them in mind. Most of the books in *The Chronicles of Narnia* are dedicated to one or more children that Lewis knew. In the case of *The Lion, the Witch and the Wardrobe*, not only does he dedicate the story to Lucy Barfield, his godchild, he states that he wrote the story especially for her. So, even though some of the ideas for the story had come about long before Lucy had been born

---

[142] *Of Other Worlds*, 23.
[143] Ibid.

(incidentally, the heroine of *The Lion, the Witch and the Wardrobe* is also named Lucy), evidently, when he wrote this story, he worked with her in mind, to please and delight her in particular. Thus Lewis's writing here is not altogether removed from a covenantal, community context. He, too, wrote for particular children, even if they were not his own.

Lewis also understood children well, having been one himself. Now this fact does not guarantee that one will understand children, for many adults either do not remember or do not want to remember much about their childhood. But Lewis did. He describes it with great perception in his autobiography, *Surprised by Joy*. Humphrey Carpenter notes the good rapport Lewis enjoyed with Tolkien's children.[144] Lewis himself tells of a wonderful moment in a restaurant when he said, out loud, 'I loathe prunes.' To his surprise, a nearby six-year old boy responded, 'So do I.' 'Neither of us thought it funny,' wrote Lewis. 'We both knew prunes are far too nasty to be funny.'[145] During World War II, Lewis took in several children who had been evacuated when the Germans were bombing London. This arrangement was the inspiration for the four children in *The Lion, the Witch and the Wardrobe*, who stay in the country house of an old professor during the air-raids. Furthermore, Lewis did enjoy a brief period of time

---

[144] Humphrey Carpenter, *J. R. R. Tolkien: A Biography* (Boston: Houghton Mifflin Company, 2000), 159.
[145] *Of Other Worlds*, 34.

as stepfather to David and Douglas Gresham, sons of his wife, Joy Davidman Lewis. 'From the very first, Jack and I were friends,' Douglas Gresham remembered. 'Jack was the exact opposite of all the "stepmothers" in the fairy tales; he was kind, jolly, and generous.'[146] Gresham remembered that at times Lewis 'would give me some pages of things he was writing and ask if I liked them. I usually did, but if I didn't, he was the kind of man who would listen to what I said.'[147] Lewis's relationship with his stepsons was apparently a good one from the beginning, for he dedicated *The Horse and His Boy* to the two brothers.

The only children's books Lewis wrote were the seven *Chronicles of Narnia*, and we will take a closer look at those books later. But these were not his only writings for children. To begin with, there is the little volume of Lewis's *Letters to Children*. Here are collected many of the letters Lewis wrote to children over the years, especially after the publication of *The Chronicles of Narnia*, when his correspondence from young readers increased dramatically. Lewis considered it his Christian duty to answer each and every letter that came to him (and there were very many, especially as his fame grew). In these letters, Lewis gives advice to children on writing, reading, and various issues related to living as a Christian (including one in which a little boy felt guilty because he

---

[146] C. S. Lewis, *Letters to Children*, ed. Lyle W. Dorsett and Marjorie Lamp Mead (New York: Simon and Schuster, 1985), 1.
[147] Ibid., 1-2.

thought he loved Aslan more than Jesus; I won't try to summarize Lewis's response here: it simply must be read[148]), as well as answering all sorts of questions about the Narnian stories.

Lewis also wrote another series of stories that have value as children's literature, especially as he wrote them when he himself was a child. These are the *Boxen* stories, and, like his *Letters to Children*, will be talked about in a later chapter of this book. *Boxen: the Imaginary World of the Young C. S. Lewis* includes stories, plays, maps, and histories of Animal-Land and India, the magical worlds created by Lewis and his brother, Warren. There are memorable characters, notably Lord Big, the frog-politician; the owl, Viscount Puddiphat; and the evil Polonius Green, a parrot. It is incredible to see the inventive imagination of these young boys, detailing the battles and political intrigues of Boxen (the union of Animal-land and India). In addition, these stories illustrate well one of the main points of this book. If Tolkien is right, that man is made to imitate his God as 'sub-creator,' then a Christian family, immersed in the Scriptures and good stories and legends, will surely bring forth the fruit of a story-telling culture, in which children invent their own worlds, their own characters; and in which fathers and mothers encourage them and add their own touches to such imaginative voyaging. When we do so, we are learning more about our God and His ways,

---

[148] Ibid., 52-53.

as well as becoming the people He wants us to be. When we refuse to do so, we are like the earth before God's creative hand touched it: 'without form, and void; and darkness was on the face of the deep.'[149]

FAMILY ACTIVITIES

1. Lewis thought the one bad way of writing for children was simply to try to give them what they want, without regard to whether the author himself is interested in such things. This he equated with talking down to children, or stereotyping them into a category, rather than dealing with them as real individuals, and thus, perhaps, not even giving them what they want, in the end. Mom and Dad: discuss together ways in which you are tempted to do the same thing. Do you find yourself thinking, 'children don't like this,' or 'children aren't interested in that,' or 'kids can't learn such things'? Can you see ways in which this kind of thinking fails to challenge children to do and learn things? Children are capable of far more than they are usually given credit for, and in any case, each child should be dealt with, not merely as a 'kid' (part of a social or demographic class) but as *your* child, a member of your family, and gifted by God with unique talents, abilities, and loves. Learn to do two things: first, challenge

---

[149] Genesis 1:2

them to go a little above their 'age', (or whatever limits the culture has declared concerning their age), and second, learn to inspire them with things that interest you. Don't simply assume that they have to have music, entertainment, books, clothing styles, and similar things, that the culture has declared to be 'age-appropriate'. Work and pray with the assumption that you will pass on your values to them, and that someday, your grandchildren will sing the same songs, read the same books, worship in the same church, and love the same God that you do now.

2. Take the time some evening to gather everyone around the fire, or the table, and teach your children something: a hymn, a poem, a passage of Scripture, a story, a catechism (the first few questions, as a start), a practical skill, or even a good joke. But it should be something of importance to you and, if possible, something that was passed on to you by *your* parents. Laugh together and enjoy this time. Let it be the first of countless *regular* opportunities to pass on the culture of Christian faithfulness to the next generation.

CHAPTER TEN

PARROTS AND POLITICS: LEWIS'S BOXEN STORIES

'What do you think of the Little-Master?' inquired the Chessknight presently.

'He's a kod,' said Green.

'Perhaps,' said Bar, 'but he's alright about some things.'

'Fer instance – ' asked Green.

'Well he didn't make me pay for those golf balls. And although he insisted on engaging in a vulgar brawl on the docks, I'm not sure that paying wouldn't have been much worse.'[150]

C. S. LEWIS, *Boxen*

I must have been around ten or twelve years old at the most. My brothers and I were ever hatching some new plot, programme, or production: spy rings, detective agencies, rock bands, war

---

[150] C. S. Lewis, *Boxen: The Imaginary World of the Young C. S. Lewis*, ed. Walter Hooper (San Diego: Harcourt Brace Jovanovich), 1985, 144.

games, always something. This time, it was an adaptation of Charles Dickens's *A Christmas Carol*, pre-booked for two sold-out appearances (the Christmas gatherings at the houses of both my paternal and maternal grandparents). The older of my two younger brothers, Chris, played Bob Cratchit, while the younger of the two, Sean, played the ghost of Christmas Past (I believed they each played a couple of other roles as well). Mom played Mrs Cratchit, and Dad filled in as the Ghost of Christmas Present. In addition, the crucial part of Tiny Tim was filled in by a younger cousin from whichever side of the family we were performing for – a different Tiny Tim each night. I was the Kenneth Branagh of the production, adapting, directing, and playing the lead role of Ebenezer Scrooge.

This masterful adaptation, which ran a good twenty minutes, including scenery and costume changes, was a big hit, and still exists on audiotape somewhere. The main thing I remember is my cousin's delivery of the one line he had as Tiny Tim ('God bless us, every one'). Only one line, no big deal. When his cue came, the little spoiler (probably around six or eight years old) blurted out, 'God bless us, ALL.'

We were not unique in doing such things. Kids love creativity, whether it be finger-painting, Play-doh sculpting, playing musical instruments, or writing stories. Even the little stories acted out before the walls of the toy castle can be wonderfully creative, and they are certainly among the best opportunities for teaching kids to play with a noble imagination.

Not all children will take their creativity to the level of fashioning an entire world, peopling it with original characters, filling it out with historical and geographical detail, and then writing short stories, plays, and novels about the land and its inhabitants. But Jack and Warnie, two brothers in the early twentieth-century, did just that. Jack, of course, is C. S. Lewis, and he and his brother Warnie (Warren) wrote their own stories and drew their own pictures to illustrate them. These stories, Lewis later wrote, 'were an attempt to combine my two chief literary pleasures – "dressed animals" and "knights in armour". As a result, I wrote about chivalrous mice and rabbits who rode out in complete mail to kill not giants but cats.'[151] One such story, 'The Relief of Murry,' was published in 1985 as part of *Boxen: the Imaginary World of the Young C. S. Lewis*. In 'The Relief of Murry,' hostile cats have surrounded Murry, the capital city of Animal-Land, on the Jemima River:

> 'Hast not heard the news from Murry?'
> 'Nay tell it me good sir,' quoth I.
> And Sir Peter said, 'The cats have beseiged Murry and it is like to fall into there hands if we do not send them help very soon.'[152]

---

[151] C. S. Lewis, *Surprised by Joy: The Shape of My Early Life* (San Diego: Harcourt, Inc., 1955), 13.
[152] *Boxen*, 37. Spelling errors in the original.

Sir Peter is 'the famous and illoustrius knighte Sir Peter Mouse,'[153] one of the main characters of Lewis's invented world, Animal-Land. Young Lewis was clearly a reader of Shakespeare, as the style of these stories shows, and he developed an early love of all things medieval, a love that would remain with him throughout his life. His brother had already begun writing stories about his own imaginary world, which he called 'India,' and the two began to collaborate in their juvenile art of sub-creation. Lewis's Animal-Land stories were medieval, but Warnie's were more modern, therefore, according to Lewis, they were 'obviously' writing about the same country in different periods of time, and the two ages had to be connected. So began the writing of the histories of Animal-Land and India. *Boxen* contains some of this history, along with notes written by Lewis on the geography of Animal-Land. There are maps, and many illustrations. The book includes a number of stories and novels, including the play, 'The King's Ring,' a mystery involving the theft of, well, the king's ring. Another piece was 'The Chess Monograph,' in which our young historian chronicles the plight of the Chessmen (yes, actual Chessmen: knights, pawns, castles, etc.: 'Just as the Jews were treated in England at the same time; so were Chessmen treated, in Animal-land...'[154]), and the building of the first Chessaries ('institutions for the lodging

---

[153] Ibid.
[154] Ibid., 50.

of Chessmen'[155]) by the famous Chess king Gengleston Herbert Flaxman.

But the heart of the book is *Boxen*, comprised of three novels ('Boxen: or Scenes from Boxonian City Life;' 'The Locked Door;' and 'The Sailor'). Here we meet the principal characters: Viscount Puddiphat, an owl; the evil Pollonius Green, a parrot; James Bar, a bear; and above all, Lord Big, a frog, who serves as Littlemaster (a combination of Prime Minister, judge, even Commander in Chief). Boxen, you see, is the political union of Animal-land and India, and is reigned over jointly by the Damerfesk (the legislative assembly) and the two monarchs of those respective countries. During the time of the novels, the two sovereigns of Boxen are Benjamin VII (a rabbit, King of Animal-land) and Hawki VI (Rajah of India). But the real power in Boxen is Lord Big, who, according to Lewis, 'brought to his task one rather unfair advantage; he had been the tutor of the two young kings and continued to hold over them a quasi-parental authority'.[156] Lewis also divulges the fact that the relationship between the young kings and Lord Big is, in fact, somewhat autobiographical, mirroring aspects of Jack and Warnie's life under their father (their mother died while they were both young, during the years of Boxen's creation, in fact). It is to the boys' credit, then, that Benjamin and Hawki are presented, not as misunderstood, noble youths, but as rather childish, irresponsible, and impetuous. In fact, they

---

[155] Ibid.
[156] *Surprised by Joy*, 80.

serve in a number of cases as a bit of comic relief, while Lord Big emerges as the central character of Boxen. In retrospect, Lewis saw Lord Big as a sort of prophetic portrait of Winston Churchill (the Boxen stories, of course, were written several decades before Churchill's emergence as the famous wartime statesman and English Prime Minister).

Big calls the kings 'boys', and chides them regularly for one thing or another. He advocates a more authoritarian approach to the kingship: 'Your fathers,' he tells them on one occasion, 'were kings in the truer sense of the word. The late rajah was not afraid to suspend from the house itself a member he disliked. Benjamin's father was known to do many such things.'[157]

If you seem to be noticing a decidedly political nature to the Boxen stories and characters, you are correct. This struck me as somewhat odd, at first. I remember having a childish interest in politics as a boy – or at least in the excitement generated by election years. But I never bothered to acquaint myself with the details and inner workings of political machinations the way young Lewis evidently did. The *Boxen* tales are filled with political power-plays, special interest manoeuvring, bribery, even duels. Many years later, in Warren Lewis's 'Memoir' (published as a preface to his edition of his brother's letters), the co-creator of Boxen revealed the source of this political inspiration as the boys' own father.

---

[157] Boxen, 92.

Mr Lewis loved to talk politics, and the topic of conversation with guests was nearly always political. 'Any ordinary parent would have sent us boys off to amuse ourselves,' Warren wrote, 'but not my father: we had to sit in silence and endure it.'[158] Warren went on to note that, in the short term, this had the effect on Jack of thinking that, in order to write in a grown-up way, he must write of politics. In the long-term, it gave him a deep disgust of anything political.

This feature, among others, makes *Boxen* somewhat unusual, when considered as children's literature. Of course, it is not children's literature in the sense of 'books written for children,' but because they were actually written *by* children, I found the stories utterly fascinating. Whether they will work as bedtime stories for your own little ones is another question. I think some of them certainly will: several of the early Animal-land tales are short and easy to follow. The Boxen novels, however, may be questionable in this regard: the plots are fairly complex, and their political nature may seem bewildering to some children. Still, it is worth a try. I think the fascination of the animal characters may overcome the very prosaic grown-up-ness of the tales, and the illustrations are certainly fun to look at. In addition, children may be more interested if they are told that little boys about their own age made up these stories.

---

[158] C. S. Lewis, *Letters of C. S. Lewis*, ed. W. H. Lewis (San Diego: Harcourt, Inc., 1966), 26.

The primary value of *Boxen*, however, lies elsewhere than in simple bedtime fare. They are a wonderful example of what Tolkien called 'sub-creation'. Tolkien saw great value in the art of literary world-fashioning. To him, myth making was the highest of all arts, for it required so much inventive energy, as the writer creates, not merely characters and plotlines, but whole worlds, with unique creatures that do not exist in the primary world. In this way, man imitates and glorifies his maker. Tolkien's understanding of myth deeply influenced Lewis, but there was a time when Lewis held a different view. He did not see that the true story of the Gospel gave a divine blessing on all secondary myths. To Lewis (at that time, anyway), myths were lies, though, as Tolkien later wrote, 'to do him justice he was kind enough and confused enough to call fairy-story making "Breathing a lie through Silver"'.[159] Tolkien's response to Lewis was to write a poem, *Mythopoeia*, on the art and value of myth-making:

> Blessed are the legend-makers with their rhyme
> Of things not found within recorded time…
> They have seen Death and ultimate defeat,
> and yet they would not in despair retreat,
> but oft to victory have turned the lyre
> and kindled hearts with legendary fire.[160]

---

[159] J. R. R. Tolkien, "On Fairy-Stories," in *Tree and Leaf: Including the Poem Mythopoeia, The Homecoming of Beorhtnoth* (London: Harper Collins Publishers, 2001), 54.
[160] Tolkien, *Mythopoeia, in Tree and Leaf*, 88-89.

Tolkien took the art of sub-creation to new heights, inventing languages, crafting detailed geography, histories, lineages, folklore, poetry, and more, all connected to his 'secondary world' of Middle-earth. I have come across nothing to indicate that Tolkien ever read the *Boxen* tales, but if he had (though surely the modern-ish, political side would not have been to his taste) I believe he would have appreciated the depth of the Lewis brothers' first attempts at sub-creation. As already mentioned, *Boxen* includes 'The Geography of Animal-Land,' as well as histories of the countries the boys created. A real attempt was made at systematising the details of the sub-creation, and developing internally consistent characters, themes, and story-lines. Furthermore, this valiant creative work was excellent training for the larger, more complex sub-creation Lewis would fashion in his later years – Narnia.

Finally, the *Boxen* stories are a fruitful example of the value of a storytelling culture. The Lewis brothers were encouraged to read by their parents, and their delight in books led them to healthy, vigorous creativity. Again, not every child is a writer. For some this creativity will find expression in painting, or playing the piano, or any number of endeavours. If to be 'godly' is to become more and more like the God we serve (though never forgetting the distinction between Him and us) then surely imitating His creativity is honouring to Him. This is what art is about, in the end: joyfully working at creating things good, true, and beautiful, for the glory of God, and the good of those made in His image.

FAMILY ACTIVITIES

1. Get the family together, preferably on a rainy Friday night, and begin creating your own literary world. Decide together what kind of world it will be. What will be the setting (contemporary, ancient past, another planet, another world entirely)? Don't write any stories at this point: just create the world. On a future occasion, you can develop characters and stories. Draw a map of the world you have made. Is it an island, or part of a larger continent? What kinds of countries surround it? What is the capital of your imaginary country? Is it well watered, with lots of rivers? Does it border an ocean? Are there mountains, plains, deserts? What kind of government rules it? Is there a king or queen? A prime minister or president? What kind of work do the people do? Is it largely an agrarian society, or more industry-driven? What is the name of your country (don't worry if you can't think of something terribly clever or exciting: 'Animal-land' is fairly ordinary).

2. On another family occasion, begin asking new questions. What kind of people and creatures will inhabit your world: men, talking animals, aliens, elves, dwarves? All of the above? If animals, what kinds of animals? Do they live together in

cities, or do cats tend to keep with cats, dogs with dogs, etc.? Now, invent a few specific characters. Perhaps, like Jack and Warnie, your children can each make up a character based on themselves. Each child can enjoy thinking of what kind of animal or other character would most fit his or her personality. Give names, backgrounds, and work to these characters.

3. Get together again, and now begin making up stories about your imagined world. Think up an exciting story that can involve everyone's character. Is there an invasion of cats (as in the Animal-land stories), or maybe a mystery to be solved? Perhaps there can be a quest for a famous treasure, or a princess to be rescued. A dragon may invade the land, or foreign armies. Be creative. The plot need not be quite so epic either: a humorous story is fun, too. Laugh and enjoy this family time together. Write the story down, if possible: at least a general outline, though if anyone in the family has writing abilities, he or she can put it in story form. Use this as a springboard for future family story-making adventures.

CHAPTER ELEVEN

HONESTY AND ENCOURAGEMENT IN LEWIS'S LETTERS TO CHILDREN

Dear Philip …,
To begin with, may I congratulate you on writing such
a remarkably good letter; I certainly could not have
written it at your age. And to go on with, thank you
for telling me that you like my books, a thing an author
is always pleased to hear. It is a funny thing that all the
children who have written to me see at once who Aslan
is, and grown-ups never do![161]

C. S. LEWIS, *Letters to Children*,
written the day before he died

'**how** many brothers and sisters would you
like?' I asked my four-year-old daughter
recently. I was exploring her views on siblings,
perhaps partly as a way to see how she has liked

---

[161] C. S. Lewis, *Letters to Children*, ed. Lyle W. Dorsett and Marjorie
Lamp Mead (New York: Simon and Schuster, 1985), 113-114.

having a little brother for the last twenty months or so.

'Ten,' she replied without hesitation.

I smiled (but not because I thought her answer silly). 'Well, Grace, if we have that many children, you'll probably be a lot older – maybe fifteen or sixteen years old – by the time they're all born, so you can help us out a lot.'

'No,' she said. 'I want to be one year old.' Her brother William is one, so perhaps she is fascinated with that age.

'But you've already been one,' I answered. 'You can't go back and be one again.'

'But,' she countered, 'Jesus said we can be born again!'

I was delighted at her response, for it demonstrates that she does listen, and remembers much. Still, I knew she had misunderstood the meaning of Jesus's words. But – please note – her mistake is the same one made by Nicodemus, a grown-up, when those same words ('You must be born again') were spoken to him by Jesus Himself. 'How can a man be born when he is old?' Nicodemus wondered. As we noted in chapter one, Nicodemus was guilty here of a failure of poetic understanding. Here is the question: is this a childish misunderstanding on the part of a grown-up (Nicodemus) or a grown-up misunderstanding on the part of a child (Grace)?

The answer is not so easy, because the line between adult and child is not as clear as some want to believe. Children are not another species, an alien race, but are human beings, albeit small and immature. Missing the poetic image of being 'born again' is a mistake that any of us can make, at any age. The solution is immersion in what Lewis called the 'right books'. Eustace, in *The Voyage of the 'Dawn Treader'*, does not recognise a dragon when he sees it, having read only the wrong sort of books.[162] Doubtless, if Nicodemus had read more books about dragons, he would not have missed Christ's point. Similarly, a child who has read the right kind of books will be better equipped to understand when God teaches us such poetic truths.

In his *Letters to Children*, a collection of some of the letters Lewis wrote in response to his many young correspondents (especially after the publication of *The Chronicles of Narnia*), just this point is made. 'I don't think age matters so much as people think,' Lewis wrote. 'Parts of me are still 12 and I think other parts were already 50 when I was 12.'[163] He said this while explaining how Peter, Susan, Edmund, and Lucy (characters from *The Lion, the Witch and the Wardrobe*) could grow up in Narnia, and become children again when they return to England.

This response defines, in a way, Lewis's approach to children. He did not view them as infants to be talked down to. As we have seen, he treated them with respect – respect for their

---

[162] C. S. Lewis, *The Voyage of the 'Dawn Treader'* (New York: Macmillan Publishing Company, 1952), 1-2, 69.
[163] *Letters to Children*, 34.

intelligence and abilities, and for their honourable status (which they share with us) as sons of Adam and daughters of Eve.[164] His letters reflect this approach. Lewis discusses literature, philosophy, and theology with children (generally based on questions they had raised themselves) in a way that would probably be more difficult for adults in our day than for children in his. He addressed questions regarding the nature of angels; the differences between myth and allegory; prayer, and more. One child asked whether Jill and Eustace (who, in *The Last Battle* are unsure of what would happen to their bodies if they died fighting for Narnia) did not know their Creed, with its insistence on the resurrection of the body. Lewis replied that while the other children in the story probably did, Jill and Eustace, who had attended a rather horrible 'progressive' government school, were probably never taught such things.

Talking to children in this way is, above all, *honest*. Where a lesser man would be tempted always to praise every artistic endeavour of a child, Lewis, while never missing an opportunity to give appropriate praise, always took the time gently to point out weaknesses in a poem or story that had been sent to him (and there were very many). An example: 'The imagery of your poem – what one can picture – is goodish. But the metre is too much of a jig for so grave a subject. Nor (forgive me!) do you handle that metre very well.'[165] Yet

---

[164] C. S. Lewis, *Prince Caspian* (New York: Macmillan Publishing Company, 1951), 211-212.
[165] *Letters to Children*, 103.

in another letter to the same girl, Lewis wrote, 'Hurrah! The essay on Easter is a promising bit of work; the sentences are clear and taut and don't sprawl. You'll be able to write prose alright.'[166] Lewis knew what all parents should know: no one is helped by pretending that children never make mistakes, or always do perfect work. By pointing out their missteps, we can help them improve in their work, or their art, and so increase their own joy as their abilities grow.

Most interesting in *Letters to Children* are the many answers Lewis gives to questions regarding *The Chronicles of Narnia*. Some are theological, like the question mentioned above regarding the Creed. Others have to do with the correct order in which to read the books: order of publication, or chronological order?[167] Still others had to do with the characters or story lines. Lewis notes in several of his letters that, for some reason, children

---

[166] Ibid, 87.

[167] When Lewis wrote *The Lion, the Witch and the Wardrobe*, he had no idea he would write any more stories of Narnia. While the first four published are chronological, the fifth book goes back to the time period covered by *The Lion, the Witch and the Wardrobe*, the sixth tells the story of the creation of Narnia, and the seventh goes forward to the last days of Narnia. Lewis said it probably does not much matter in which order they are read, but that chronological is probably best. Having read the series many times, often with any number of senseless orders, I can say that, for a first reading, order of publication is best (there are interesting things to discover by reading, say, *The Magician's Nephew* after *The Lion, the Witch and the Wardrobe*). Chronological order would probably be best for a second reading, and after that, it truly does not matter. One can touch down at any point in Narnian history and find new wonders with each reading.

almost always understand the deeper Christian significance of the books, while adults rarely do. Here he explains the way the Christian themes of the book work: 'I'm not exactly "representing" the real (Christian) story in symbols. I'm more saying "Suppose there were a world like Narnia and it needed rescuing and the Son of God (or the 'Great Emperor oversea') went to redeem it, as He came to redeem ours, what might it, in that world, all have been like?"'[168]

Lewis encouraged his young correspondents, many of whom were aspiring writers, and he often gave them practical advice on writing. One of the most interesting bits of creative advice he gave had to do with the Narnian stories themselves. After the seventh and final book was published, many children wrote, asking if there would be more. Lewis replied that he was sorry to say there would not, that he had said all he had to say about Narnia, and that, after all, it is better to leave readers wanting more than to make them tired of the whole thing. But, he suggested (to a number of children), why not make up your own stories of Narnia? He had given hints, he said, of other stories and characters that are only mentioned, but never developed. These could be the starting place for many additional stories of Narnia, Archenland, Calormen, or the Lone Islands. Such hints are a mark of a great storyteller, who, from time to time, casts momentary glances at other untold tales within his

---

[168] *Letters to Children*, 92.

own tale. We are reminded that, no matter what part of the story we are reading (whether the story of Narnia or the stories of our own lives and people we have come to know) that there is always much more going on than we can possibly see. Our lives are perhaps a paragraph each in the great Story that God is telling. The mystery of the unknown tales is meant, I believe, to set our imaginations racing at the infinite ways of our storytelling God. St John tells us this: 'And truly Jesus did many other signs in the presence of His disciples, which are not written in this book.'[169] Indeed, John tells us, 'there are also many other things that Jesus did, which if they were written one by one, I suppose that even the world itself could not contain the books that would be written.'[170] There is always more to the story, just as Lewis's *Letters to Children* tells us more of the story of Narnia, and of C. S. Lewis himself. Perhaps, as our children make up new stories about Narnia, or about their own imagined worlds, they are learning that all of us, every day we live, are helping to tell God's great Story of Jesus Christ to the world. May we do so with grace and holiness.

FAMILY ACTIVITIES

1. Mom and Dad: set aside a time to talk together about your children and the way you

---

169 John 20:30
170 John 21:25

communicate with them. It is easy for any of us to slip into the habit of talking down to children, because they are young and immature. Certainly we want to enjoy their childhood, but (and this is especially important in a culture like ours, that glorifies perpetual adolescence) we should strive to set 'growing-up' before our children's eyes as a good and worthwhile goal to strive for. Read *Letters to Children* and see if there is anything to learn, both in the expectations Lewis has of young intellects, and in the manner he communicates to them. Practise speaking to your children in ways that communicate love and respect, while also understanding the real limitations of childhood. Refusing to talk down to children does not mean talking to them just as you would an adult, and it certainly doesn't mean deliberately peppering conversations with words and ideas they cannot understand. It *does* mean recognising that they are capable of far more than we have been conditioned to think, and showing the proper respect for their God-given abilities and desire to learn.

2. If everyone is so inclined, get together and write a letter to your favourite author. I imagine many, if not most, writers, would feel encouraged to hear from their young readers. Include a picture based on the story, if you wish, and talk about the themes, characters, and story of the book. The letter can be written from the entire family, and you never know what results this might yield. The Kilmers, a family of American children, began

writing to Lewis regularly about the Narnian stories, and Lewis eventually dedicated *The Magician's Nephew* to them!

3. Finally, Mom and Dad should get together and write their own letter to their children. Write a letter to each child, or one single letter with parts addressed to each child. Talk to them about the things that make them special, the things that make you smile. Talk about their talents, their strengths, their weaknesses. Talk about your dreams for them – not so much the 'I want you to be a rich doctor' dreams, as the 'I want you to be a godly man or woman with a noble heart and a Christian imagination' dreams. Perhaps you haven't written stories like *The Chronicles of Narnia* that you can discuss with them, but you can discuss the story of your own family. You can (as both a character, and, in a secondary way, one of the storytellers) explain to them what some of the pictures, symbols, battles, and plot twists of *that* family story mean.

CHAPTER TWELVE

THE ADVENTURE THAT ASLAN SHALL SEND US: THE SOVEREIGN GOD OF LEWIS'S THE CHRONICLES OF NARNIA

...When I started The Lion, Witch and Wardrobe I don't think I foresaw what Aslan was going to do and suffer. I think He just insisted on behaving in His own way. This of course I did understand and the whole series became Christian.[171]

C. S. LEWIS, *Letters of C. S. Lewis*

He's wild, you know. Not like a tame lion.[172]

C. S. LEWIS

The Lion, the Witch and the Wardrobe

The Old English poem *Beowulf* was perhaps the most influential work of literature in the

---

[171] C. S. Lewis, *Letters of C. S. Lewis*, ed. W. H. Lewis (San Diego: Harcourt, Inc., 1966, 1988), 486.

[172] C. S. Lewis, *The Lion, the Witch and the Wardrobe* (New York: Harper Collins Publishers, 1950), 180.

life and work of J. R. R. Tolkien. C. S. Lewis, too, knew and loved it, and taught it to his students at Oxford (his 'Beowulf and Beer' nights were legendary and much loved). That epic poem tells us a story that resonates with the theme of divine sovereignty over the affairs of men. Take these words, for instance, spoken by Hrothgar, king of the Danes, for whom Beowulf had just killed the monster, Grendel:

> For the sight I see to the Sovran Ruler
> be speedy thanks! A throng of sorrows
> I have borne from Grendel; but God still works
> wonder on wonder, the Warden-of-Glory.

God's sovereign rule over the world is seen in *Beowulf* in the use of the word *Wyrd*. If that word sounds – weird, that is because it is exactly where we get our modern English word, 'weird'. But here it means 'destiny', or even 'history', 'what has happened', and it refers, in certain key respects, to God's control over all events in our lives, even when we cannot figure out what He is doing. As an example, Grendel's evil days are cut short by *Wyrd*:

> Then laughed his heart;
> for the monster was minded, ere morn should dawn,
> savage, to sever the soul of each,
> life from body, since lusty banquet
> waited his will! But Wyrd forbade him
> to seize any more of men on earth
> after that evening.[173]

Wyrd forbids Grendel from working more evil on the Danes, though the poet, as we have seen, attributes the wicked creature's downfall 'to the Sovran Ruler'. *Wyrd*, then, is a word used by the poet to signify a sense of divine destiny, the plans of a sovereign God whose will cannot be thwarted.

The sovereignty of God is a touchy subject in many parts of Christendom. Debates over predestination and election mark a dividing line between otherwise co-belligerent Christians. My theological background is that of the Reformed faith, and, as such, I have rather definite views on the subject. In times past, while debating the issue, I would have recommended to those who disagree with me any number of books by popular Reformed theological writers. While I still see much value in such books, my approach today is somewhat different. These days, I am inclined to suggest, to those who want to better understand the sovereignty of God, such literary works as *Beowulf*, *The Chronicles of Narnia*, George MacDonald's *At the Back of the North Wind*, or *The Zeal of Thy House*, by C. S. Lewis's friend, Dorothy L. Sayers.

The last work, in particular, makes very strong statements on the issue. *The Zeal of Thy House* is a play that dramatises the rebuilding of the cathedral of Canterbury by William of Sens. As the

---

[173] These quotes are from the modern English translation of *Beowulf* by Francis B. Grummere. Public domain, released July 1993. The entire text can be found online at www.fordham.edu/halsall/basis/beowulf.html

play opens, the monks of Canterbury are deciding, among several architects, which shall be the man to rebuild the cathedral choir. The angels Gabriel, Michael, Raphael, and Cassiel are watching over the proceedings. Michael wonders aloud whom the monks shall choose. 'They will choose the man whom God has appointed,' replies Cassiel. 'I shall see to it that they do,' says Gabriel. He whispers in the ear of the last of the monks to vote (and who is evidently fast asleep), 'William of Sens.' The old monk casts his vote for William, and one of the other monks shouts at him that he has not heard a word that was said. 'You needn't shout,' replies the tired monk. 'I'm not deaf. I have followed everything very carefully. I said William of Sens and I mean William of Sens.'[174]

Notice the words Sayers puts in the mouth of the holy angel: 'They will *choose* the man whom *God has appointed*,' (emphasis added). Both man's legitimate choice and God's sovereign determination are proclaimed, not as contradictions, or 'parallel lines that meet in eternity', but as the one (human choice) ultimately depending on the other (God's free determination). Though Sayers was no Calvinist, this is well in keeping with the Reformed *Westminster Confession of Faith*, in which we are told that God ordains whatever comes to pass, yet in such a way that both secondary causes and

---

[174] Dorothy L. Sayers, *The Zeal of Thy House* (London: Victor Gollancz Ltd, 1937), 26, 28.

the will of the creature are established. We may not fully understand this; we must affirm it to be true.

We see this same balance in *The Chronicles of Narnia*. Aslan – who, in this 'supposal', as we discussed earlier, is Christ as He might have been in a world such as Narnia – guides his subjects with what can only be described as a sovereign determinism. In this chapter, we will take a closer look at Lewis's view of God, and of His leading in the lives of His people, as revealed in the world of Narnia.

First, though, for those who are perhaps unfamiliar with the stories, let us take a few minutes to provide an overview of the books. Please note: in order to discuss these books, crucial plot points, even the endings, must be revealed.

The first book – chronologically – is *The Magician's Nephew*, which tells the story of the creation of Narnia. Digory, a boy from the country who has had to move to London because his father is abroad and his mother dying, meets a girl named Polly. While exploring one day, they find themselves in the study of Digory's Uncle Andrew, a self-styled magician. Uncle Andrew tricks Polly into touching a magic ring, which sends her right out of the world. Uncle Andrew had been experimenting with a magic box given him by his godmother, old Mrs LeFay. The box contained dust from the lost city of Atlantis, and from it Uncle Andrew had made the rings. Digory has no choice but to take a ring himself and try to find Polly. The two children find themselves in the dying world of Charn, where Digory unwittingly (and yet because of a foolish choice) awakens Jadis, the White Witch, from an enchanted sleep. Through a series of strange twists, the children, the Witch, Uncle Andrew, and a London cabbie and his horse, Strawberry, end up in Narnia on the day of its creation. Aslan is singing, bringing the new world to life with His song. Because Digory had brought the Witch to Narnia, Aslan sends him on a mission to retrieve an apple from a tree in a garden far away (from the apple, Aslan will plant a tree that will protect Narnia from the Witch). While there, in a scene deliberately evocative of the Garden of Eden, Digory is tempted by the Witch to eat the apple, or to take it for his dying mother, for whom it could doubtless bring healing. Digory refuses the temptation, and brings the fruit back to Aslan as ordered, with joyful and unexpected results.

The Lion, the Witch and the Wardrobe, though the first book written and published, is the second in chronological order. Four brothers and sisters, Peter, Susan, Edmund, and Lucy, find their way into Narnia by way of a magic wardrobe – a wardrobe, as readers of *The Magician's Nephew* will know, that was made from a tree grown from the seeds of the apple Digory had brought to Aslan. In Narnia, they find that the White Witch, Jadis, has returned, and has had all Narnia in a spell of perpetual winter for a hundred years. Edmund betrays them to the Witch, and the children meet Aslan, who has come back to Narnia to battle the

Witch. The Witch lays claim to Edmund's blood for his treachery, a claim Aslan does not deny. In the end, she releases her claim on Edmund's life, but only because Aslan has agreed to take his place. In a scene reminiscent of both the Garden of Gethsemane and of Christ carrying his cross to Golgotha, Aslan, accompanied by Susan and Lucy, goes to the Stone Table, where He is slain by the Witch. The next morning, however, Lucy and Susan find that He has risen from the dead, a miraculous and joyful turning point that the Witch could not have foreseen. Aslan and the girls go to the Witch's house (in a scene inspired by the phrase in the Apostle's Creed, 'He descended into Hell'), and sets free those whom the Witch had turned to stone. Then Aslan and his new army of former statues race to help Peter and Edmund, locked in a bitter battle with the Witch's forces. The Witch is slain, peace is restored, and the four children are crowned by Aslan to rule as Kings and Queens in Narnia.

The Horse and His Boy takes place during the reign of Peter, Susan, Edmund, and Lucy in Narnia. Shasta is a boy being raised by a cruel fisherman named Arsheesh in Calormen, a land to the south of Narnia. Upon finding that the fisherman plans to sell him to a Calormen nobleman (a *Tarkaan*, as they are called), and on finding that the Tarkaan's horse, Bree, is a talking horse of Narnia, Shasta and the horse run away together, trying to get out of Calormen and to 'Narnia and the North!' Along the way they meet Aravis (a Tarkheena, a daughter of a Tarkaan) and her horse, Hwin, another talking horse who, like Bree, had been captured and taken from Narnia years before. The four journey together to the great city of Tashbaan, where Shasta meets King Edmund, Queen Susan, and other Narnians (they mistake him for Prince Corin of Archenland, who was travelling with them). Before Shasta is able to rejoin his friends, Aravis learns that Prince Rabadash of Calormen is planning a secret attack on Archenland (neighbour and ally of Narnia), and the horses and children race across the desert, trying to get to the city of Anvard ahead of Rabadash to warn King Lune of Archenland. In the end there is a great battle. Shasta meets Aslan, and finds that he (Shasta) is really Prince Cor of Archenland, twin brother of Corin (which is why he was mistaken for him), and in fact, heir to the throne. The book evokes a powerful sense of longing for another land – a longing all Christians understand well. It deals particularly with the theme of suffering and trials, and the meaning they have in our lives.

In *Prince Caspian*, the four children return to help Caspian, the rightful heir to the throne, defeat his usurping Uncle Miraz. Those of 'old Narnia' – including dwarfs, fauns, centaurs, and talking beasts – have long been in hiding, with the result that the men of Narnia think them only old wives' tales or nursery stories. But Caspian had always believed in them, and when he has to go into hiding to avoid being murdered by Miraz, he finds old Narnia, and leads them into battle. *Prince Caspian* is a powerful story with themes of loyalty, faith, and the restoration of joy in a sorrowful world.

Lucy and Edmund return to Narnia, along with their cousin Eustace, in *The Voyage of the 'Dawn Treader'*, a seafaring tale. They journey with Caspian to the Lone Islands and beyond, searching for the seven lords, loyal to Caspian's father, who had been sent on a voyage to the world's end in order to get them out of Miraz's way. Many adventures befall Caspian and the children, and one of the main threads of the story is the conversion of Eustace, a horrible, self-centred boy, into a faithful friend and servant of Aslan. Eustace, through his greed and selfishness, is turned into a dragon, and, seeing very clearly his own nature for the first time, begins to have a change of heart. But he finds he can do nothing to take away his dragon-nature, and must rely wholly on the power of Aslan to do this work of grace in him (more on this later). Eventually, along with their shipmates, and Reepicheep the Mouse (one of the best-loved characters in the Narnian books) they do reach the world's end, and Aslan appears to them, in one of the most obviously Christ-centred passages in the series, as a lamb. He also cooks a breakfast of fish for them, just as Jesus did for the disciples.[175] He promises that He will meet them in their own world and that they would know Him there by another name. Indeed, He reveals to them that knowing Him better in

---

[175] John 21:9-13

our world was the whole reason they had been brought to Narnia, and readers may safely infer that this is the whole reason *they* have been brought to Narnia as well.

The Silver Chair finds Eustace in Narnia again, this time with Jill, a friend from school. Jill meets Aslan himself in his own country, and he gives her and Eustace the mission of finding the lost prince of Narnia, who has been missing for ten years. She is given four signs to look for along the way – signs that will show them they are on the right path. Along with Puddleglum, a Marsh-wiggle of Narnia, they set off to find the lost prince. For various reasons (all brought on by the poor choices of the children) they miss the first three signs. The fourth – that someone would ask them to do something in the name of Aslan – does not come at all as they expected, and they are forced to make a terrible choice: obey, and risk danger and possible death, or do what *seems* right, and remain in safety. When the Prince is found, he, along with the children and Puddleglum, face the reality of powerful spiritual deception in the enchantments of the witch who had held the Prince captive all these years. This is one of the best passages in the entire series, in my opinion, and shines a brilliant light on the virtues of truth, goodness, and beauty, perhaps more brilliantly than anything else Lewis ever wrote. There is also, in the character of Puddleglum, a wonderful picture of unassailable faith and loyalty, even in the face of despair and darkness. Though I waver on this, I often think *The Silver Chair* is my favourite of the seven Narnian books.

Finally, *The Last Battle* chronicles the story of Tirian, 'last of the kings of Narnia who stood firm at the darkest hour'.[176] 'Darkest hour' is appropriate for this edge-of-your-seat story. It is a dark tale, full of great sorrow and loss. The grief and terror are best expressed in words that are spoken twice, each time by a different person: 'If we had died before today we should have been happy.'[177] *The Last Battle* is Lewis's story of the end of the world, complete with an anti-Christ figure (an ape who has dressed a donkey in a lion skin, making the creatures of Narnia believe that Aslan has returned) and an apocalyptic final battle (Narnia's own Armageddon). At last, Aslan brings judgment on His enemies, makes an end, shuts the door, and night falls on Narnia. But Tirian, Eustace, and Jill – and Peter, Edmund, Lucy, Polly, and Digory, who all return in this final story[178] – learn that nothing good is ever finally lost, and that Aslan's own country is more glorious and beautiful than they could possibly have imagined. Scriptural imagery and themes abound in this book, and there is also a Bible story told in miniature in *The Last Battle*. This is nothing unusual: Lewis's writings are filled with

---

[176] C. S. Lewis, *The Last Battle* (New York: Macmillan Publishing Company, 1956), 146.
[177] Ibid, 20.
[178] If you're wondering why Susan is not mentioned here, you will have to read *The Last Battle* to find out.

this sort of imaginative re-telling (the story of the Garden of Eden in *Perelandra*; the Tower of Babel in *That Hideous Strength*; the crucifixion and resurrection of Christ in *The Lion, the Witch and the Wardrobe*), usually with a creative twist, but this is one I only recently noticed. It involves King Tirian. Notice some key facts about his story:

1. He is of the royal house in a great country.
2. His people have become enslaved by a foreign power.
3. He sees a slave-driver beating one of his countrymen.
4. He flies into a rage and kills the slave-driver.
5. He flees for his life.
6. This act causes him to lose his noble and royal position.
7. He returns to lead his people to freedom.

Sound familiar? It should, for it mirrors the story of Moses as recounted in the book of Exodus. But remember: Lewis usually adds a twist when incorporating these Biblical narratives into his fiction. In this case, the twist involves the entrance into the 'Promised Land': Aslan's Country. Moses is forbidden (at least for the time being) to enter the Land, but Tirian, in this apocalyptic reversal, does enter the Land. Of course, the Land he enters is the True Narnia, of which the Narnia of Tirian's world (and the Canaan of Moses's world) is but a type and a shadow. Through Aslan (Christ, the greater New Covenant counterpart to Moses), we have been guaranteed entrance into that Country by faith alone.

Thus the stories of *The Chronicles of Narnia*. Perhaps even in this brief recounting you can begin to see the theme of divine sovereignty which runs throughout the seven books. If the forest as a whole shows this characteristic mark, then the trees surely will. Let us look at some of the trees, then.

What I have begun to see as in many ways the main theme of the Narnian stories is found in both the first book written (*The Lion, the Witch and the Wardrobe*) and the last (*The Last Battle*). In the first, near the end, Peter, Susan, Edmund, and Lucy, now grown up, and having reigned in Narnia for years, are pursuing the famous White Stag, who will give wishes if caught, it is said. Suddenly they come upon a lamp-post in the middle of a wood.[179] Though they had all seen the lamp-post years before, when they first came to Narnia, they have all but forgotten their life in this world, remembering it only as a dream. So they decide to carry on, though they all sense that passing the lamp-post will bring about some great change in their lives, and Susan says, 'let us go on and take the adventure that shall fall to us.'[180] In *The Last Battle*, we find this same idea, but more definite and better understood, I think, than Susan's words: 'Tirian said they could come with him and take their chance – or, as he much more

---

[179] For the story and significance of the lamp-post, see *The Lion, the Witch and the Wardrobe* and *The Magician's Nephew*.

[180] C. S. Lewis, *The Lion, the Witch and the Wardrobe* (New York: Harper Collins Publishers, 1950), 204-205.

sensibly called it, "the adventure that Aslan would send them".'[181] Elsewhere Tirian again says, 'we must go on and take the adventure that comes to us'.[182] Tirian's ancestor of more than two hundred years before, Rilian (the prince rescued by Eustace, Jill, and Puddleglum in *The Silver Chair*) said the same thing: 'let us descend into the city and take the adventure that is sent us.'[183]

Notice the progression of the idea, more and more specific throughout the series: Susan says they should take the adventure that 'falls' to them, almost as if in a random, chance fashion. For Rilian, they are to take the adventure that is 'sent' them, showing clearly that he believed that whatever dangers and sorrows befell them were events directed by a sovereign hand (it is worth noting that he said this just after proclaiming, 'Aslan will be our good lord, whether he means us to live or die. And all's one for that.'[184]). And Tirian is the most specific, stating plainly that the adventures they would take were not only sent, they were sent by Aslan Himself.

Think what this means: if the adventures are 'sent', they must be guided by a Hand capable of bringing about complex, detailed, specific events in history. This implies that even the free choices of many, many individuals – the Witch, the gnomes

---

[181] *The Last Battle*, 94.
[182] Ibid, 20.
[183] C. S. Lewis, *The Silver Chair* (New York: Macmillan Publishing Company, 1953), 168.
[184] Ibid.

of Underland, the ape, the men of Calormen, just to name a few – are also divinely guided. Does this mean our actions are really not free, that we are merely puppets? Lewis clearly did not believe that, any more than Sayers when she had the angel say, 'They will choose the man whom God has appointed.' Still, the sovereign hand of God is undeniable to those who know the Scriptures. Here are just a few:

Whatever the LORD pleases He does,
In heaven and in earth,
In the seas and in all deep places
(*Psalm 135:6*).

The king's heart is in the hand of the LORD,
Like the rivers of water;
He turns it wherever He wishes
(*Proverbs 21:1*).

All the inhabitants of the earth are reputed as nothing;
He does according to His will in the army of heaven
And among the inhabitants of the earth.
No one can restrain His hand
Or say to Him, 'What have You done?'
(*Daniel 4:35*).

But as for you, you meant evil against me; but God meant it for good…
(*Genesis 50:20*).

For truly against Your holy Servant Jesus, whom You anointed, both *Herod and Pontius Pilate*,

> with the Gentiles and the people of Israel, *were
> gathered together to do whatever Your hand and
> Your purpose determined before to be done*
>   (*Acts 4:27-28*, emphasis added)

Notice especially the last passage: Herod, Pontius Pilate, along with all those who killed Jesus, did 'whatever [God's] hand and [God's] purpose determined before to be done'. Though it is not so explicitly stated in *Narnia*, the same idea is everywhere assumed. In *The Magician's Nephew*, Aslan tells his newly-created talking beasts that an evil witch has entered their land. Still, he tells them: 'Evil will come of that evil, but it is still a long way off, and I will see to it that the worst of it falls upon myself.'[185] This is both prophecy and sovereign determinism, as Aslan declares, many hundreds of years in advance, the certainty of the evil choices of the witch, as well as the outcome of them.[186]

---

[185] C. S. Lewis, *The Magician's Nephew* (New York: Macmillan Publishing Company, 1955), 136.

[186] Of course, I am not suggesting that God is somehow to blame for the evil choices of His creatures. And it should be pointed out that Lewis, in *Mere Christianity*, suggested a philosophical solution to this perennial problem (that is, if God knows in advance the choices we will make, do we have the freedom to choose otherwise?). For Lewis, God, outside of time, sees the past and the future in the same way He sees the present, for all are before His eyes as a single moment. He does not, according to Lewis, go through time (except in Christ's incarnation) and so it is not so much that He foresees free choices, as that He merely sees them. Past, Present, and Future are all the same to Him. Just so, in *Narnia*, Aslan says, 'I call all times soon' (*The Voyage of the 'Dawn Treader'*, 138). Either way, God determines what will happen,

In *The Lion, the Witch and the Wardrobe*, Peter, Susan, and Lucy, deeply troubled over their brother Edmund's treachery, as well as the terrible danger he is in, ask Aslan if nothing can be done to save Edmund. 'All shall be done,' replies Aslan, 'But it may be harder than you think.'[187] Again, the foreknowledge of Aslan is clear, including the certainty of Edmund's salvation.

In *The Horse and His Boy*, one of the clearest pictures of divine sovereignty is painted. Throughout his journey out of Calormen, Shasta is beset by many troubles: he and his friends are chased by lions on several occasions, including one in which Aravis had been injured by a lion. Shasta had nearly lost his friends in Tashbaan, and had had to go on alone, after Aravis was wounded and the horses spent, to finish the journey and warn King Lune of Archenland of the approaching Rabadash. Finally, he is lost in the fog, separated from the king, and nearly overwhelmed by despair, now thinking himself the most unfortunate boy that ever lived. A voice out of the mist says to him, 'I do not call you unfortunate.' Shasta replies that, at least, it was terrible luck to meet so many lions. But the voice replies, 'There was only one lion.' In response to his wonder at this, the Voice then tells him, 'I was the lion.' He was indeed the lion who had chased them at the beginning of the journey, forcing them to join with Hwin and Aravis. He had been

---

using even the free choices of human creatures to accomplish His will. As Joseph said in the Scripture quote above, "you meant evil against me; but God meant it for good."

[187] *The Lion, the Witch and the Wardrobe*, 141.

the cat who comforted the lonely Shasta, waiting for his friends outside the tombs near Tashbaan. He was the lion who chased away the jackals that same night. He was the lion who again chased Shasta and his friends, causing fear in the horses that gave them the speed they needed to reach King Lune in time. 'And I was the lion,' the Voice continues, 'you do not remember, who pushed the boat in which you lay, a child near death, so that it came to shore where a man sat, wakeful at midnight, to receive you.' Notice that all the sad events of Shasta's life, including the one that led to his terrible childhood in the home of Arsheesh, were designed and brought about by Aslan for a better purpose than Shasta could possibly have realised. Shasta also sees however that, if this lion were the only lion they had met, then he was also the one who had wounded Aravis. 'It was I,' the Lion responds. But he will not tell Shasta why He had done this, for, He says, He 'tells no one any story but his own'.[188]

This is a theme that will resurface in some of the other Narnian stories, and it shows clearly that the best way for the characters to understand their lives is as a story – a story that Aslan is both telling, and writing. The story itself is beautifully suggested for us in *The Voyage of the 'Dawn Treader'*. In a book owned by Coriakin, an old man who is actually a star,[189] Lucy reads a beautiful story. It

---

[188] C. S. Lewis, *The Horse and His Boy* (New York: Macmillan Publishing Company, 1954), 158-159.
[189] In Narnia, stars are actually people. When they are too old to shine in the sky any longer, they 'retire,' as Edmund put it, and appear as human beings. In this they do not get older, but

is three pages long[190] and by the end of the first
page she forgets that she is reading at all. The
story becomes her story and she is living in it. At
the end of the story she is quite overwhelmed by
it, and realises that it is the most beautiful tale she
has ever heard. She decides to read it again, but
the book's pages cannot be turned backwards. At
least, she thinks, she must remember the story,
but it is fading from her mind already. All she can
recall is that the story was about a cup, a sword,
a tree, and a green hill. Aslan appears shortly
thereafter and she asks him if he will tell her the
story. 'Indeed, yes,' Aslan says, 'I will tell it to you
for years and years.'[191] Again we see that it is Aslan
who tells the story. It has been suggested, and
with good reason, that the story Lucy read is the
biblical story of redemption. The cup is the cup
of the New Covenant of which Jesus said, 'This is
my blood.' The tree is the cross on which He died,
and the hill is the hill on which His death won our
redemption. And the sword? Kathryn Lindskoog
suggested that it might be the sword Peter took
up to defend his Master in Gethsemane.[192] But

---

younger, and when they have returned to the age of a newborn
baby, they ascend into the sky once more. Coriakin is not actually
a 'retired' star, but a star who had been commissioned by Aslan
to govern a very foolish people called the Duffers (later the
Dufflepuds), as a punishment.
[190] Suggesting, perhaps, the Trinity, or the Three Days that
culminated in Christ's resurrection.
[191] C. S. Lewis, *The Voyage of the 'Dawn Treader'* (New York:
Macmillan Publishing Company, 1952), 136.
[192] Kathryn Lindskoog, *Journey Into Narnia* (Pasadena, California:
Hope Publishing House, 1998), 150.

perhaps it has a different meaning. Jesus Christ, as Lewis knew, was the archetype for all dragon-slayers. Christ threw down Satan, the dragon, by His death and resurrection. But the mythological dragon-slayers, whether Beowulf, St George, or Bard (from Tolkien's *The Hobbit*) always use a weapon of some kind – in many cases, a sword. Perhaps the sword of Lucy's story is meant to remind us – in the context of the cup of Christ's blood, and His death on the tree on a hill – of the greatest dragon-slayer of all. So Lucy is taken into the story of Christ, and it becomes her story, as she embraces it and believes it.

Aslan is represented as the Lord of Narnia's history, and the keeper of Narnia's people. In *Prince Caspian*, Lucy asks Aslan what would have happened had she followed him the first time she saw him, instead of going with the others, who could not yet see him. He tells her that no one is ever told what *would* have happened.[193] He repeats this to her after a similar question in the house of Coriakin in *The Voyage of the 'Dawn Treader'*.[194] The implication is, nevertheless, that what would have happened is something that *can be told*. This only makes sense, though, if there is a Mind possessing all knowledge, and Aslan is presented as just such a Mind.

Aslan, mirroring Christ, is sovereign over the lives of both His people and His enemies – and

[193] C. S. Lewis, *Prince Caspian* (New York: Macmillan Publishing Company, 1951), 137.
[194] *The Voyage of the 'Dawn Treader'*, 136.

over their salvation. There are several pictures of redemption in the Narnian stories, and all make the case that salvation is in greater hands than of those who actually need it. In *The Voyage of the 'Dawn Treader'*,[195] Eustace, as already mentioned, becomes a dragon, a clear symbol of the sinful nature all of us possess. He longs to be transformed, to no longer be a dragon, but he cannot make this happen. He meets Aslan who tells him to 'undress'. Eustace begins to scratch away at the scaly dragon-skin, and finally succeeds in tearing it off. But there is another dragon-skin underneath. He does it again, and again finds another skin. A third effort throws him into despair, realising that he cannot go deep enough to un-dragon himself. Finally, the Lion plunges his claws into Eustace, causing terrible pain, so that Eustace thinks his heart has been pierced. But Aslan tears away the horrible dragon scales, and restores Eustace to his former self – well, not really, for the selfish, bratty Eustace is gone, replaced by a new Eustace: brave and thoughtful, though still imperfect. In this story, Eustace cannot save himself, nor can he even make himself want to be saved. It takes a terrible event – being turned into a dragon – to bring himself to realise his need. Everything good that happens to him comes from outside of him. As Martin Luther once said, 'The Gospel is completely outside of you.'

---

[195] Pp. 86-92.

In *The Silver Chair*,[196] Jill sees Aslan for the first time. She does not know who he is, and is afraid of him (rightly so). Her throat is burning with a terrible thirst, but the Lion is lying right in front of the stream from which she wants to drink. He invites her to come and drink, but she is afraid. She asks if he will promise not to do anything to her, but he will make no such promise. She wonders if he does in fact eat girls. He responds by telling her that not only has he eaten girls, but boys, men and women, kings, emperors, cities, realms. She decides to find another stream. 'There is no other stream,'[197] says the Lion. Finally, Jill, terrified, does drink. The Lion then calls her to come to him. Does he eat her? One could say he swallows up her old self. He would not promise not to 'do anything' to her – did he do something to her? Yes – he called her to himself, changing her forever. Before they came to Narnia, Eustace had told Jill about his previous adventures with Caspian, King of Narnia. Then he and Jill called on the name of Aslan (whom she knew nothing about yet) to ask him to let them come to Narnia. Later, after Jill drinks from the Lion's stream, he speaks to her of the task for which he had called them into Narnia. Jill is convinced he is mistaken – after all, she says, no one called them into Narnia: it was they who had done the calling. Aslan replies: 'You would not have called to me unless I had been calling to you.'[198]

---

[196] Pp. 14-18.
[197] *The Silver Chair*, 17.
[198] Ibid, 19.

Notice the strong divine hand in bringing Jill to Aslan. Coming to Aslan in the Narnian stories – for those who come with trust and humility – is always a redemptive experience, parallel to one's conversion to Christ, for in coming to him, one comes to believe in him and love him. This happens repeatedly in the series: Peter, Susan, and Lucy coming to Aslan in *The Lion, the Witch and the Wardrobe*; Trumpkin coming to Aslan (after many loud pronouncements of unbelief) in *Prince Caspian*; Shasta and Aravis (at different times) meeting Aslan in *The Horse and His Boy*; Digory and Frank the Cabbie in *The Magician's Nephew*; and Emeth in *The Last Battle*. Of course, many come to Aslan, not with trust and love, but with faithlessness and hatred: Uncle Andrew and Jadis in *The Magician's Nephew*; Prince Rabadash in *The Horse and His Boy*; the dwarfs in *The Last Battle*. It really is arguable that one of the most important themes of the books is that of coming to Aslan, in one way or another. One of the final scenes in the series is of a time when all the creatures of Narnia, small and great, come to him – some look into his eyes with love, and pass through the door into his country, while others look with hatred and fear, passing into his shadow, never to be heard from again.

Aslan also shows himself sovereign, not only over the lives and redemptions of his people, but over their deaths as well, thus showing that he has the power of both life and death. In *The Magician's Nephew*, he gives to Digory a fruit that brings healing to his mother, who is ill and near death's door. In *The Lion, the Witch and the Wardrobe*, he gives his own life, only to take it up again in resurrection. In *Prince Caspian*, Aslan comes to a dying old woman. 'Oh, Aslan!' she says, 'I knew it was true. I've been waiting for this all my life. Have you come to take me away?' Aslan replies to her: 'Yes, dearest,' he says. 'But not the long journey yet.'[199] Then he heals her and raises her up. 'Not the long journey yet' – Aslan tells her she will die someday, but not yet. He brings her back from death's door because it was his good pleasure to do so. In *The Voyage of the 'Dawn Treader'*, the children ask how to get into his country from our world. He will not tell them whether the way is long or short, 'only that it lies across a river. But do not fear that, for I am the great Bridge Builder.'[200] The river is death, clearly, and they are told not to fear it. The Bridge Builder will take them across the river, and note the significant beginning of this statement – 'I am.' This is the covenant name of God (Yahweh; see Exodus 3), which Aslan will speak again only a few paragraphs later. In *The Silver Chair*, Rilian declares that Aslan will be their good lord, 'whether he means us to live or die. And all's one for that.'[201] Notice here that it is Aslan who either means them to live or die, and notice also Rilian's almost carefree indifference as to which it is, resting wholly in the will of his

---

[199] *Prince Caspian*, 197.
[200] *The Voyage of the Dawn Treader*, 215.
[201] *The Silver Chair*, 168.

good Lord. Earlier in the book, Aslan had told Jill to search for the Prince until she had either found him, gone back into her own world, or died in the attempt. And at the end of the book, the aged Caspian has died. His dead image appears in the stream in Aslan's country, while Jill, Eustace, and even Aslan stand by, weeping. Aslan bids Eustace pluck the large thorn from a nearby thicket and drive it into his paw. Eustace does so, and a large drop of blood splashes into the stream over the dead king. Then Caspian changes, until he is the young king Eustace had known long ago. He leaps up, very much alive, and there is a great reunion. Eustace is overjoyed, but concerned that Caspian is only a ghost, since he has died. Aslan responds that Caspian has indeed died. 'Most people have you know. Even I have. There are very few who haven't.'[202] But Caspian assures Eustace that he has come into his own country now, and a man cannot be a ghost in his own country. Again we see life and death in the paws of the great Lion, and a crystal clear image of salvation and life through the blood of the Saviour. (Later, in *The Last Battle*, Aslan is described as 'the good lion by whose blood all Narnia was saved.'[203]) And of course, in *The Last Battle*, the theme of death runs everywhere, from Tirian's lament that they would have been happy if they had died before the great sorrows befell Narnia, to Eustace and Jill

---

[202] Ibid, 213.
[203] *The Last Battle*, 33.

wondering what would happen to them if they died in Narnia; from Roonwit the Centaur's dying words that 'noble death is a treasure which no one is too poor to buy,'[204] to the final realisation of the Professor (Digory), Polly, Peter, Edmund, Lucy, Eustace, and Jill that the reason they are in Aslan's country is because they have already died in a railway accident. Therefore, Aslan tells them in some of the most moving words in all literature, 'The term is over: the holidays have begun. The dream is ended: this is the morning.'[205] From beginning to end, the Lion rules over all – time and space, salvation and judgment, life and death.

Like all his fiction, Narnia is merely the incarnational enfleshment of his biblical and theological beliefs. Lewis believed strongly in the sovereign grace of God in salvation (though he could not be labelled a Calvinist, he did have a high view of predestination). In his work English Literature in the Sixteenth Century, he describes the early Protestant doctrines of grace (and though he is here wearing his literary critic's hat, not his theologian's, only the most cynical could deny the obvious sympathy he has for those doctrines). Lewis says, 'All the initiative has been on God's side; all has been free, unbounded grace... He is not saved because he does works of love: he does works of love because he is saved. It is faith alone that has saved him: faith bestowed by sheer gift.'[206]

---

[204] Ibid, 91.
[205] Ibid, 183.
[206] C. S. Lewis, English Literature in the Sixteenth Century Excluding Drama (London: Oxford University Press, 1954), 33.

Not only is salvation a gift; even the faith necessary to take hold of that salvation is 'sheer gift'[207].

The Chronicles of Narnia, like all great works of literature, is a vast and deep ocean, with wonders behind every wave. No essay or book can explore all those depths, and what we have done here is merely take our little boat a few miles out from shore. The mark of a truly good book is surely that it yields new insights, previously overlooked, on each new re-reading. In his *Experiment in Criticism*, Lewis maintained that good books could be known by the kind of readers they attract, and particularly whether readers make life-long companions of them, reading them time after time over many years.[208] The Narnian stories are great books: books to return to over and over again with our families through the years. My own children are very young, but we are reading through *The Chronicles of Narnia* with my daughter now, and I hope to read these books many times to my children and, God willing, my grandchildren some day. They are simply indispensable – modern classics, not only a revival of, but a great leap forward (along with the books of Tolkien) for the traditional fairy story. When a Christian writer achieves such a thing, it is simply not to be missed.

---

[207] I am indebted once again to Douglas Wilson for pointing out the significance of this passage in his fine article 'Was C.S. Lewis Reformed?' (*Credenda Agenda*, Vol. 13, Issue 5: 'Jack: A Reformed Appreciation of C.S. Lewis').

[208] C. S. Lewis, *An Experiment in Criticism* (Cambridge: Cambridge University Press, 1961), 1-2.

FAMILY ACTIVITIES

1. Read *The Chronicles of Narnia* as a family (if you can, get the large *Complete Chronicles of Narnia*, a great family book, with the original black and white illustrations brought to colourful life by Pauline Baynes, who drew the original pictures). Lewis said that children almost always understood the deeper meaning of Narnia, while adults almost never did. See if this proves true for your children. Ask them pointed questions: what do you think of Aslan? A good place to begin this is in *The Lion, the Witch and the Wardrobe*, where Lewis describes the way each of the children felt after hearing the name of Aslan for the first time. Of course, at this point, none of the children (including your own) know who he is. Ask them who they think he might be. Then, as the story progresses, perhaps as you finish a chapter at night (Lewis wrote the chapters of nearly equal length for ease of reading aloud), have further discussions. Find out if the death and resurrection story seems familiar. Ask them also what other thoughts came to mind as they heard the story – perhaps there will be insights that they pick up on that you overlooked. Guide them (more by questions than outright statements) to some of the points they may have missed. Look for the Christian imagery and ideas and see if they ring any bells with your children. A few examples would include: Shasta (in *The Horse*

and His Boy) asking Aslan who he is, and Aslan responding by saying 'Myself' three times and in three different ways; the scene in *The Voyage of the 'Dawn Treader'* in which Aslan appears as a lamb; Aslan's creation of Narnia and the garden scene in *The Magician's Nephew*; the signs Jill and Eustace are given in *The Silver Chair*; and the false Aslan in *The Last Battle*.

2. During the course of your reading, have a sort of party – for you and your children, or for others as well who may be interested – with a Narnian theme. Don't turn it into a mini-Star Trek convention, with the kids dressed up like Aslan and the Witch (no better way to surrender the mystery and majesty of the Lion than to turn him into a Halloween costume). The point of this party is to highlight the stories, so my suggestion is, the simpler the better. The main thing to do, apart from reading the stories, is to prepare Narnian food for the evening. Pick up Kathryn Lindskoog's wonderful book *Journey Into Narnia* (Hope Publishing House). The second section of the book, 'Exploring the Narnian Chronicles,' includes sections that talk about the food from each book, sometimes including recipes. She even has a recipe for the enchanted Turkish Delight that led Edmund astray in *The Lion, the Witch and the Wardrobe*, and the name she gives to the recipe – 'Turkish Delight for Greedy Fools' – reminds us of the evil way in which Jadis and Edmund made use of it. Most of the ideas are simple, including 'really

good grapes' as were eaten in *Prince Caspian*, or baked apples, as in *The Silver Chair*, though there are many other ideas as well. Other than that, spend some time in the week or so before the party creating Narnian-themed works of art, much as you did with *The Hobbit*. Decorate the living room (or wherever) with the pictures, sculptures, poems, or stories you made earlier. Have an evening of reading and discussion. You could also look into buying a few copies of the dramatic adaptation of *The Lion, the Witch and the Wardrobe* (Oberon Books, dramatised by Adrian Mitchell) and go through it in 'reader's theatre' fashion, with each person reading the part for a different character. Have fun – if a family's storytelling culture is not enjoyable, something is wrong.

CONCLUSION:

THE CONTINUING STORY: LIFE IN THE GREAT FAIRY TALE

All tales may come true; and yet, at the last, redeemed, they may be as like and as unlike the forms that we give them as Man, finally redeemed, will be like and unlike the fallen that we know.[209]

J. R. R. Tolkien

throughout this book, I have written from the belief that Lewis and Tolkien were essentially correct in their understanding of the Christian story as the true myth, the fairy tale that came true. I have found this idea to be controversial among Christians, however; so a few more thoughts are perhaps in order.

One criticism that has been levelled at mythology by conservative Christian critics has to

---

[209] J. R. R. Tolkien, "On Fairy-Stories," in *Tree and Leaf: Including the Poem Mythopoeia, The Homecoming of Beorhtnoth* (London: Harper Collins Publishers, 2001), 73.

do with the otherworldly creatures of fairy tales, whether Tolkien's elves, dwarves, and dragons, or Lewis's giants, centaurs, fauns, and witches. Some see such things as silly juvenilia, unworthy of the adult Christian mind ('When I became a man, I put away childish things,' as St Paul wrote). Others suspect a more diabolical twist, with fauns and elves no more than demons in disguise. As to the latter condemnation, we may notice that such beings, in classical literature, and particularly in Lewis's Narnian stories, are not necessarily spirits at all, but physical, earthly creatures. Some literary figures – dragons and witches come to mind – are universally symbolic of evil, and can only be turned from this purpose with unavoidable moral confusion. But centaurs, fauns, elves, dwarves – these are much closer to human beings, in the sense that some humans are wicked, haters of God, and some are noble, redeemed creatures, though still fallen, who may hope, in the grace of their Creator, to do some good. Just so, a faun need not automatically be thought demonic, just because of its appearance in classical, pagan mythology – after all, humans appear in those stories, too.

As to the charge of silliness or immaturity, one can only wonder how often such critics read their Bibles. As we noted earlier, the Bible is full of fantastic, sometimes otherworldly creatures: giants, witches, unicorns, talking animals, angels, and dragons. It is *possible* to see *some* of this as merely symbolic – we don't imagine Satan really has scaly skin and wings, for example – but we cannot escape the fact that this is the way God chose to tell His story. Many Christian books these days are strong on spiritual ideals and practical tips, but dreadfully 'weak on dragons',[210] as Lewis put it. But why? If the Bible uses a plethora of literary styles, including poetry, apocalyptic visions, and, as we have argued, fairy tales, why should not we learn from the Master Communicator, and the all-time best-seller? If we are truly longing to reach the world with our message, surely we can learn something from the fact that the two best-selling books of the twentieth century were the Bible and *The Lord of the Rings*. Please note, I am not arguing that since mythology 'sells' we should adopt it as a context for the Gospel. My argument is based on the fact that the Bible uses this kind of story and imagery to teach us, and we ought to imitate the Bible more.

Further, it is because the Bible has this 'fantasy' element (even though it records absolutely true history) that we can enjoy fairy tales and mythology. Perhaps it is even a good intellectual or spiritual exercise, for truly, if we think fairy tales silly, we ought to think the Bible even sillier. 'Never since the world began has it been heard that anyone opened the eyes of a man born blind.'[211] Who ever heard of such strange happenings? We are forced to admit that, by modern standards, the Bible is an exceptionally weird book. It assaults the modern mind by its very supernatural character. Without

---

[210] C. S. Lewis, *The Voyage of the 'Dawn Treader'* (New York: Macmillan Publishing Company, 1952), 71.
[211] John 9:32 (ESV).

the slightest bit of irony or allegory, with no tongue
in cheek, we are asked to accept such things as,

> Then Joshua spoke to the LORD in the day when the
> LORD delivered up the Amorites before the children
> of Israel, and he said in the sight of Israel:
>
>> 'Sun, stand still over Gibeon;
>> And Moon, in the Valley of Aijalon.'
>> So the sun stood still,
>> And the moon stopped,
>> Till the people had revenge
>> Upon their enemies.
>
> Is this not written in the Book of Jasher? So the
> sun stood still in the midst of heaven, and did not
> hasten to go down for about a whole day. And
> there has been no day like that, before it or after
> it, that the LORD heeded the voice of a man; for
> the LORD fought for Israel.
>
> (Joshua 10:12-14).

God creates the universe with a word, He divides
the sea in two, He rains fire from Heaven at the
prayer of his prophet, He makes wine from water,
He raises the dead. This is the God we serve, the
Faith we are called to embrace and believe. Is it
not more otherworldly, more fantastic, far greater
than the most miraculous fairy story? And so the
strange creatures of Fairy-land, Narnia, or Middle-
earth are worth reading because they force us to
ask ourselves: 'if this is too much to believe, how
shall I ever believe the Holy Scriptures?'

We are also forced to deal with the reality
that Lewis and Tolkien, in writing their fairy tales,

were, in the end, writing about *this* world. After all, it is this world that is the arena of the Bible's extraordinary events. Tolkien's tales take place in a mythical antiquity of our own world, as (within the confines of his imagined legendarium) a definable epoch of our own history. It was, after all, a myth for England he was crafting. In addition, in the Narnian stories, we see hints of this relationship between the world of Narnia and our world. In *The Voyage of the 'Dawn Treader'*, as mentioned before, Aslan reveals that he is in our world as well, with another name. Significantly, Lewis sets the third volume of his Space Trilogy, *That Hideous Strength* – which he subtitles, *A Modern Fairy-Tale for Grown-Ups* – entirely in this world, and in Lewis's own time.

Fairy stories are not allegories, but they do point, in a symbolic way, to life in this world. Christ threw down the Dragon in this world. The Dragon is still seeking to devour us, in this world. Therefore, we are called to be (in a secondary, derivative, and imitative way) dragon-slayers, here in this world. Many have loved ones who have fallen into folly and evil. As we grieve for them, how do we understand their dire situations? Were they not enticed by some sin, some device of the enemy made to look attractive, appealing, and innocent, like Snow White's apple (or the fruit of the Tree of the Knowledge of Good and Evil)? When they took the bait, and fell into the Enemy's thralldom, is it not true that they fell under the spell of a diabolical enchantment? Now this is not to say that they were somehow lured against their will, hypnotized as it were, so that they are not morally responsible. They were enticed by the attractiveness of the spell, and were overthrown by their own choice, made with eyes wide open. But this is precisely what enchantment *is*. Those who try to define enchantment in a way that absolves them of responsibility should heed the words of Aslan to Digory in *The Magician's Nephew*. Digory, explaining to Aslan why he rang a bell in a hall of witchcraft – with the result of bringing the White Witch into the new land of Narnia – tries to excuse his actions by saying he thinks he was a bit *enchanted* by the writing on the bell. 'Do you?' asks Aslan in a voice that makes it clear He already knows the answer. The question is enough to open Digory's eyes. 'No,' he wisely admits. 'I see now I wasn't. I was only pretending.'[212] In *that* sense, no one is enchanted; yet when we give in to sin, we become captives, slaves to it, and this is very much like being under a spell. We should see ourselves as engaged in the great task of breaking the Dragon's evil spells. This is a task that only God can accomplish, but He has called us to be a part of that noble work.

The work of fighting the Dragon, and breaking his evil spells, requires a measure of heroism and courage not common in the modern world. Dangers and desperate quests may await us

---

[212] C. S. Lewis, *The Magician's Nephew* (New York: Macmillan Publishing Company, 1955), 135.

around every corner, with every tick of the clock. G. K. Chesterton's brilliant amateur detective, Father Brown, once remarked, 'I never said it was always wrong to enter fairyland. I only said it was always dangerous.'[213] We must fight, nobly and heroically, even when defeat and doom (in the temporal sense) are certain. We are not guaranteed long life or unending happiness in this world. In *The Silver Chair*, Aslan tells Jill that she and Eustace are to search for the lost prince until they have either found him or died in the attempt, and he makes no promise as to which will happen. In *The Lord of the Rings*, Eomer, king of Rohan finds himself surrounded by his enemies, facing certain death and downfall. How does he respond? 'And lo! even as he laughed at despair he looked out again on the black ships, and he lifted up his sword to defy them.'[214] This must be our confidence when the armies of darkness press around us, drunk with the wine of many victories, and all hope seems gone. We fight on, knowing that even if *we* are conquered, God's kingdom never will be, and that some day even Death itself, the last enemy, will be swallowed up in victory. This is what fairy tales teach us, and it is what the Scriptures teach as well. Hebrews 11 chronicles the great heroes of the faith, who, among other things, 'subdued kingdoms, worked righteousness, obtained

---

[213] G. K. Chesterton, *The Complete Father Brown* (London: Penguin Books, 1981), 105.
[214] J. R. R. Tolkien, *The Lord of the Rings: The Return of the King* (New York: Ballantine Books, 1965), 122.

promises, stopped the mouths of lions, quenched the violence of fire, escaped the edge of the sword, out of weakness were made strong, became valiant in battle, turned to flight the armies of the aliens' (vs. 33-34). Yet we are told that these noble heroes 'did not receive the promise' (v. 39). They were conquered, in one sense, and did not live to see the final victory. But they knew it would come, and they fought the Dragon to their last breath.

They did so through faith, knowing there was more going on than meets the eye. In a decidedly mythical (though also historical) passage, the armies of the Syrians have surrounded Dothan, the town where the prophet Elisha lives. Elisha's servant cries out in despair, 'Alas, my master! What shall we do?' Elisha prays that the servant's eyes will be opened: 'And behold, the mountain was full of horses and chariots of fire all around Elisha.'[215] We are not alone in our battles.

But we must at least be aware that there *is* a battle. Many Christians have laid down their arms, never striking a blow. This is tempting, especially when all seems to be going well in life. Sometimes we forget the nature of the Dragon, and are tempted to let down our guard. Christopher Robin (of *Winnie the Pooh* fame) has some good advice for us here, as he engages in 'Rushings-Out, and Rescuings,'

And Savings from the Dragon's Lair,
And fighting all the Dragons there.
And sometimes when our fights begin,

---

[215] II Kings 6:15-17

I think I'll let the Dragons win …
And then I think perhaps I won't,
Because they're Dragons, and I don't.[216]

If ever we are tempted to let the dragons win, we should recall the reason to keep fighting: 'Because they're Dragons.' If you ask my four-year-old daughter what she knows about dragons, she will say, 'dragons don't listen to God.' She knows they are evil. But dragons, a universal symbol for evil (see Revelation 12), are often portrayed as soft, friendly, or misunderstood creatures in our day. Popular children's shows like *Dragon Tales* reinforce this inversion of the true tradition of fairy stories. We know better, however. 'Dragons cannot be tamed, and it is fatal to enter into dialogue with them,' writes Michael D. O'Brien in his indispensable book, *A Landscape With Dragons: The Battle for Your Child's Mind*, 'The old stories have taught our children this.'[217] O'Brien helpfully discusses the symbolic image of the dragon throughout the history of literature, and points out the moral problems with 'friendly' dragons. In Scripture, dragons destroy and devour, and confusion in young minds will be the result if we then present them with Puff the Magic Dragon, or the noble Draco from the movie *Dragonheart*. Besides, the traditional way is more interesting. 'At least in the old days dragons looked and acted

---

[216] A. A. Milne, *Now We Are Six* (New York: Dutton Children's Books, 1927), 53.
[217] Michael D. O'Brien, *A Landscape With Dragons: The Battle for Your Child's Mind* (San Francisco: Ignatius Press, 1998), 33.

like dragons,' O'Brien writes. 'A landscape with dragons is seldom boring.'[218] Again, we must talk about dragons to our children, teaching them the true nature of the Dragon, our enemy.

Here we have a tremendous opportunity to reinforce the truth of the Bible with our little ones, and we have only ourselves to blame if we do not. As we discussed in Chapter One, God expects us to read, and to read books other than the Bible. We read devotional books that imitate the teaching approach of the apostle Paul: why not read books that imitate the story-telling of Jesus, or John? Such are fairy tales. Faith, courage, loyalty, nobility, miracles: many elements of the true faith are present in these tales. We talked about the need for valour in the face of overwhelming odds. How can we find such bravery? Because we remember that the 'highest function' of fairy tales, according to Tolkien, is the 'happy ending'. We know that God has already written the end of the tale, and that it will be glorious, and joyful indeed. This is reason enough to press on through our discouragement and grief; reason enough to make the effort to create a story-telling culture in our home, knowing that there is no better way to build godly character in our children. May God bless us in this, and raise up our sons as knights of the Kingdom, our daughters as valiant princesses of the High King.

And may the Dragon and his armies know the bitter taste of downfall and ruin, to the glory of God.

---

[218] Ibid, 65.